Revisiting Keynes

Revisiting Keynes
Economic Possibilities for our Grandchildren

edited by Lorenzo Pecchi and
Gustavo Piga

The MIT Press
Cambridge, Massachusetts
London, England

For information about special quantity discounts, please email special_sales@mitpress.mit.edu

This book was set in Palatino on 3B2 by Asco Typesetters, Hong Kong.
Printed and bound in the United States of America.

Library of Congress Cataloging-in-Publication Data

Revisiting Keynes: economic possibilities for our grandchildren / edited by Lorenzo Pecchi and Gustavo Piga.
    p.   cm.
Includes bibliographical references and index.
ISBN 978-0-262-16249-4 (hbk. : alk. paper) 1. Keynesian economics. I. Pecchi, Lorenzo, 1957– II. Piga, Gustavo, 1964–
HB99.7.R48   2008
330.15′6—dc22   2007045991

10 9 8 7 6 5 4 3 2 1

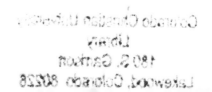

to Alma and Ivo
to Niccolò

Contents

Contributors

William J. Baumol
New York University

Leonardo Becchetti
University of Rome Tor Vergata

Gary S. Becker
University of Chicago

Michele Boldrin
Washington University in Saint Louis

Jean-Paul Fitoussi
Institut d'Études Politiques de Paris

Robert H. Frank
Cornell University

Richard B. Freeman
Harvard University

Benjamin M. Friedman
Harvard University

Axel Leijonhufvud
University of California in Los Angeles

David K. Levine
Washington University in Saint Louis

Lee E. Ohanian
University of California in Los Angeles

Lorenzo Pecchi
UniCredit Group

Edmund S. Phelps
Columbia University

Gustavo Piga
University of Rome Tor Vergata

Luis Rayo
University of Chicago

Robert Solow
Massachusetts Institute of Technology

Joseph E. Stiglitz
Columbia University

Fabrizio Zilibotti
University of Zurich

Acknowledgments

We wish to thank all those who encouraged us in this endeavor from day 1: Robert Solow, who gave us the kind and confident push we needed at the start, and all those who followed and gave value to our initial intuition, paying tribute to the eloquence of John Maynard Keynes, even when opposing his views and philosophy.

John Covell, at The MIT Press, was a strong believer in the project all the way. Thank you. We thank also an anonymous referee and Dana Andrus for her superb editing. Silvia Ceccacci, Nicole Dunaway, Alessandro Marchesiani, Merila Murillo Pecchi, Paolo Paesani, and Barbara and Henry Slayter provided very much needed support.

The chapters of this book, written by so many renowned economists, are a reminder of the future our grandparents fought to leave us with, and an admonishment to keep on fighting for our grandchildren just as they did. As such, it is a book meant for this generation and this generation alone.

Economic Possibilities for our Grandchildren: A Twenty-first Century Perspective

Lorenzo Pecchi and Gustavo Piga

The idea for this book materialized one evening, as we were talking on the telephone about a short essay written by John Maynard Keynes in the early 1930s, *Economic Possibilities for our Grandchildren*. In the space of a few pages Keynes formulated a series of fascinating and daring predictions on social life and economic conditions one hundred years on, giving almost the impression of wishing to challenge posterity to put his predictions to test. This was a tempting challenge indeed, coming from a man considered by many as the greatest economist of the twentieth century, and a mighty challenge too, given the number and nature of the questions raised in the essay and their potential to generate lively debates and passionate disagreement.

It came natural to us to share this idea with other economists and to ask them to give their opinion of Keynes's short essay by writing one of their own. We contacted many leading economists, some of whom, we knew, would be well disposed toward Keynes's opinions and some of whom, we expected, would oppose them. Some of those we contacted politely rejected the offer, but we received sixteen affirmative responses from some of the most celebrated economists in the world: William Baumol, Leonardo Becchetti, Gary Becker, Michele Boldrin, Jean Paul Fitoussi, Robert Frank, Richard Freeman, Benjamin Friedman, Axel Leijonhufvud, David Levine, Lee Ohanian, Edmund Phelps, Luis Rayo, Robert Solow, Joseph Stiglitz, and Fabrizio Zilibotti.

This book collects their essays in addition to Keynes's own. It is a book about growth, inequality, wealth, work, leisure, culture, consumerism, and entrepreneurship, offering a variety of perspectives on where the *Economic Possibilities for our Grandchildren* stand at the start of the twenty-first century and presenting the reader with many fascinating new questions and answers, hopefully as fascinating and powerful as the original ones.

According to Keynes's biographer Robert Skidelsky, *Economic Possibilities for our Grandchildren* (*Economic Possibilities* from this point on) has been generally considered by economists as no more than a *divertissement* (Skidelsky 1992). We do not have any direct records of how much Keynes valued this particular piece of work, but we are convinced that he was particularly fond of the ideas presented in the essay, and that they should therefore be considered as a small but important clue to his way of thinking.

The first version of *Economic Possibilities* dates back to the beginning of 1928. After delivering it a few times, mostly as a talk to students' societies, Keynes undertook some major revisions for a lecture to be given in Madrid in June 1930, adding a specific reference to the oncoming Great Depression. The final version of the essay, which appears reprinted in this book, got included in Keynes's 1931 *Essays in Persuasion*.

By 1930 Keynes was convinced that he and his contemporaries were witnessing a very deep economic crisis. On May 10 he wrote in *The 'Nation'*: "The fact is—a fact not yet recognized by the great public— that we are now in the depth of very severe international slump, a slump which will take its place in history amongst the most acute ever experienced. It will require not merely passive movements of bank rates to lift us out of the depression of this order, but a very active and determined policy." (Harrod 1972, p. 469). Despite the difficulties of the time Keynes refuted the "bad attack of economic pessimism" prevailing at that moment in many economic circles and did not feel the need to alter his optimistic view about the long-term prospects that capitalism was supposed to deliver. Finally he included *Economic Possibilities* in his 1931 *Essays in Persuasion* collection.

Economic Possibilities contains three relevant elements (1) a remarkably modern account of the determinants of economic growth, (2) a set of predictions concerning living standards and working habits one hundred years on (i.e., in 2030), and (3) some speculations about people's future lifestyles, based on his moral philosophy and aesthetical views.

The contemporary reader will be surprised both at how accurate some of his predictions on income levels turned out to be and at how off the mark he was when speculating about working hours and future lifestyles. As to this particular point, he predicted that, by 2030, the grandchildren of his generation would live in a state of abundance, where satiation would be reached and people, finally liberated from such economic activities as saving, capital accumulation, and work would be free to devote themselves to arts, leisure, and poetry.

Despite substantial economic growth between 1930 and the present—not to mention the exceptional achievements in such fields as medicine, biochemistry, transportation, computing and telecommunication—nothing today looks farther away than the world envisioned by Keynes (even if twenty-five years are still separating us from the time when his prophecy is supposed to take place). Keynes's grandchildren are wealthy indeed and even wealthier than he had forecast. But they still have to save and to accumulate and work long hours, and they do not seem to have reached satiation in consumption. How could it be that a man of Keynes's intelligence, with a deep understanding of economics and society, could be so right in predicting a future of economic growth and improving living standards and so wrong in understanding the future trends of labor and leisure, consumption, and saving?

Keynes's Forecast on Growth

Keynes's prophecy that "the standard of life in progressive countries one hundred years hence will be between four and eight times as high" turned out to be right or, if anything, wrong by default. As calculated by Zilibotti in this book, "Keynes's forecast implies an upper bound growth rate of about 2.1 percent. The population-weighted average growth rate over the half-century in question is 2.9 percent per year, implying a 4-fold increase in the standards of living in just *fifty years* .... If the 2.9 percent annual growth is projected over one century, it corresponds to a 17-fold increase in the standards of living, amounting to more than double Keynes's upper bound."

Making such predictions in England in the 1930s would not have been obvious for at least two reasons. First, ever since the start of World War I, growth had been very slow—far from increasing, per capita income had actually slightly decreased—and, what is more important, growth was much lower than during previous decades (Boldrin and Levine, chapter 12 of this book), making it too gloomy a setting for optimistic predictions. Second, economists then did not have many tools to make theoretically sound predictions about growth: "Growth theory—as we know it today—did not exist in the 1930s. There was little in the way of theory that would lead an economist of that era to predict confidently a steady state growth path in which output remains close to its long-run trend. The Harrod-Domar model that was developed in the 1930s predicted that market economies were unstable, with chronically high unemployment and that steady states were knife-edge propositions." (Ohanian, chapter 6 of this book).

In *Economic Possibilities for our Grandchildren*, Keynes, generally acclaimed for his contribution to business cycle theory, proves to be a superb growth theorist well aware of the mechanics of economic development: capital accumulation and technical progress. Keynes did neglect aspects of the growth process that could not be imagined then: the prospects for global climate change, which is today an important economic issue given the scale of the costs that it may impose on society or "the growing availability of weapons of mass destruction at bargain prices"—as William Baumol reminds us in this book—that may seriously impair our future prosperity. But he also neglected details about growth that could have attracted his attention: the lack of universal improvement in the standards of living, both within and across countries, its possible fragility due to inappropriate government policies and the reversal in social and political arrangements, like democracy, if living standards were to start stagnating once more.

Keynes's Forgetfulness about Distribution

Keynes's main concern in writing *Economic Possibilities* was the future of those grandchildren living in the so-called progressive countries, namely Europe and North America. The least we can say is that he had a manifest ethnocentric view and that he did not pay much attention to the destiny of the rest of the world. Data presented by Zilibotti in this book show how growth has been very different over time and various geographical areas. In Europe, per capita income growth was very high in the 1950s and 1960s, slowing down afterward. In North America, the opposite occurred, with per capita income growing moderately in the 1950s and 1960s and picking up later in the next decades. Japan and other Eastern Asian countries suffered quite a lot in the 1990s, while India and China have experienced an exceptional growth in the last two decades. Latin American countries presented a strong economic performance in the third quarter of the century and later went through a series of crises. A similar destiny awaited North African and Middle East countries. Unfortunately, no significant progress was made by sub-Saharan Africa in the last 50 years. On average then, humankind has been able to progress in line with Keynes's most optimistic expectations. Income distribution, however, remains a problem that, as more than one author in the book points out, Keynes utterly overlooked.

As Stiglitz recalls in this book "some 50 percent of the world still lives on less than two dollars a day, some one billion still live on less than a dollar a day." To this it might be added that not only do we see extremely poor countries next to affluent countries (cross-country inequality) but also extremely poor individuals living next to rich individuals both in developed and developing countries (within-country inequality). This aspect is here emphasized by Friedman who provides data about the increased inequality in the United States in the last quarter of the century concluding that the "more unequal distribution had prevented the great majority of the nation family from any increase in real terms."

In many industrialized countries we observe a larger and larger portion of income concentrating in the hands of capital owners and highly skilled workers (human capital owners) with a considerable increase in their living standard while living standards of unskilled workers are stagnating or growing very slowly. This brings about an interesting issue regarding the relationship between wages and economic growth. Keynes's forecast is based on the assumption that with technical progress and increasing capital–labor ratios, wages will always increase. He does not pay attention to distributional issues and their consequences.

This view is challenged by Robert Solow who, having stated that "Keynes's utter lack of interest in distributional matters is a serious flaw," goes on to argue that "the distribution of income and output between wages and profits depends on the ease with which capital can be substituted for labor. . . . If this kind of substitution is relatively easy, profits will come over time to absorb an ever-increasing share of aggregate income. Wages will also rise, but not enough to keep up with profits." The extreme case is one of a society where the production is performed almost entirely by machines or robots. In this case the share of wages would be close to zero, and workers could survive only if they own capital. These distributional scenarios were not contemplated by Keynes, but in a not too distant future they could belong more to reality than to science fiction. Some of these trends are already showing up in the data. Society will have to solve some complex political issues. An increasing degree of inequality may result in a deterioration of the necessary social cooperation required by a well-functioning society. A solution to this situation—as Solow suggests—

is to have institutions that guarantee a more democratic capital ownership.

Keynes on Hours Worked

A society where production is largely robotized is a society where humankind works very little and has a lot of free time. This is what Keynes predicted, though in his mind the choice of leisure over labor would have resulted from a rational calculation. This was another daring forecast that Keynes expressed in the *Economic Possibilities* essay: an income effect caused by increasing real wages would lead individuals to substitute leisure for labor, a superior good, to the point that the normal working week would be of only fifteen hours.

A significant reduction in the number of hours worked was well in place at the end of the nineteenth century and in the first decades of the twentieth: the average annual number of hours worked per worker fell by almost 30 percent between 1870 and 1930, both in Europe and the United States. Ohanian shows that Keynes's prediction could be justified on the basis of macroeconomic trends around the years Keynes was writing. But this declining trend slowed down strongly in the aftermath of World War II, particularly in the United States.

While it is true that the fraction of an individual's lifetime spent on working activities is much smaller today than in 1930 (Zilibotti), it is also true that, as Freeman says in his essay, "The United States is the most striking counterexample to Keynes's prediction that increased wealth would produce greater leisure. The United States has 30 to 40 percent higher GDP per capita than France and Germany, but employed American work 30 percent more hours over the year than employed persons in those countries." "The decision of Keynes's grandchildren to work so much," he continues, "is associated with a reversal of what had been an historic inverse relation between hours and pay. In past decades the poor have worked more than the rich. They had to work long and hard to feed themselves and their families. Work or perish. The rich, by virtue of their land holdings or hereditary position in society, could be idle if that was their fancy. The phrase idle rich had real meaning. In the latter half of the twentieth century, the inverse relation between hourly pay and hours worked reversed itself, at least in the United States. The workaholic rich replaced the idle rich. Those earning higher pay worked more hours than those earning lower pay."

Why do we work more than Keynes predicted? The question is not irrelevant even for policy purposes as the debate is nowadays raging, for example, as to why these differences exist on the two sides of the Atlantic. Several factors are at play and are laid out in this book by our contributors. We briefly cite just a few.

First of all, Keynes might have underestimated the pleasure of working. As Freeman argues in his essay, "Many people go to work for reasons beyond money, and might prefer to work longer than Keynes's fifteen hours a week under almost any situation. Workplaces are social settings where people meet and interact. On the order of 40 to 60 percent of American workers have dated someone from their office."

A similar argument is put forward by Phelps who focuses on the figure of the entrepreneur: Keynes conveyed no sense of the role of innovations in imparting excitement and personal development to business careers. "...nowhere does Keynes recognize the wisdom of the pragmatic school—from James to Dewey to Rawls and on to Sen—that people need to excite their minds with novel challenges—new problems to solve, new talents to develop.... So, were working-age people not to work or to work only a few hour a week, a great number of them would find themselves deprived of the fruit that is the special prize of the most advanced economies."

Increased participation of women to the workforce after World War II compensated for the reduction in working hours by men. Inequality and globalization also might have induced individuals to work more. Freeman argues that "greater inequality enlarges the earnings gap between greater/lesser success in the market and thus gives workers more incentive to work long hours to succeed." Also, he argues, "the advent of the computer and Internet make it easier for many people to work away from their offices."

Becker and Rayo argue that "Keynes was misled in his predictions concerning the effect of higher income on hours worked by the behavior of gentlemen in Britain—who Keynes believed provided a window onto future behavior as everyone's income rose. Their behavior gave a distorted picture of what to expect because these gentlemen had sizable wealth in the form of physical and financial assets, but not high human capital or earnings. So economic theory would predict that these gentlemen would take more leisure than would equally wealthy persons in the future who in fact would be holding the vast majority of their wealth in human capital, rather than land and other assets. English gentlemen indeed had mainly just an income effect, while those

who have to work for their high incomes also have powerful substitution effects. This difference is illustrated by the working habits
of wealthy individuals in the various Gulf States, who typically get
the vast majority of their income from oil revenues. It is said that in
many of these countries, such as the Emirates, Qatar, or Kuwait, the
typical working day for natives—as opposed to the imported laborers
who do not share in oil revenues—is about three to four hours a day.
This is actually very close to Keynes's estimate of how many hours
would be worked in advanced countries after another century of economic growth."

But Keynes was twice wrong. He claimed not only that work would
disappear but also that additional consumption needs, beyond the
"basic ones," would not materialize. Baumol reminds us in his essay
that if Keynes were to have been right in his working hours forecast,
humanity would have responded to the increase in prosperity less
in output growth and more in "immeasurable psychic and aesthetic
pleasures. . . ." In this case humanity could not have experienced the
explosion of output, innovation, and consumption that we have had in
the last century. This would have deprived us of an interesting thought
experiment, since now we can imagine what kind of luxuries an average western citizen will have at her disposal if real income will once
again increase sevenfold in the next century!

Keynes on Conspicuous Consumption

Keynes's idea of a virtuous steady state where robotized production
provides for all human necessities without the need for capital accumulation and technological progress contained a final ingredient: stable consumption and no (or little) saving.

Consumption satiation and the end of technological innovation
(whether through capital deepening or new discoveries) were thus
in Keynes mind two self-sustaining dimensions of life in the quasi-
proximate future. He was wrong on both counts. Both Frank and
Friedman, for example, argue that while satiation might occur for
increasing doses of a given type of product, the sheer mass of new
products created since the 1930s (air conditioners, television sets,
home computers, washing machines for both dishes and clothes)
thanks to efforts of innovating entrepreneurs might themselves create
new desires and new demands by consumers. This in turn requires
increasing doses of human effort. Indeed, if this is the case, Frank

argues, "it is hard to imagine that a two-hour workweek might some-day enable most people to buy everything they ever wanted."

In his essay Keynes distinguished among "absolute needs," what we feel "whatever the situation of our fellow human beings might be," and "relative needs," what we feel only insofar as they make us "feel superior" to our fellow citizens. He discarded this last cause of consumption in his successive reasoning, as if to imply it was an unimportant component.

In the book, however, several authors forcefully argue that Keynes neglected many facets of what motivates consumption in a human being. Fitoussi takes issue with the notion of absolute needs, arguing that as their satisfaction is conducive to social inclusion, they change over time together with the evolution of society. Much in the same vein, Leijonhufvud and Becker-Rayo argue that medical care has expanded with technology, becoming that vastly superior good that motivates people not to be satiated with consumption. Friedman seems to endogenize the concept by arguing that growth (especially the impressive one correctly forecast by Keynes himself) brings about vast improvements in the social, political, and moral character of people. Growth may therefore also contribute to the evolution of the concept of basic needs.

Other authors recognize that Keynes did not dwell enough on the concept of consumption desires that are relative. He certainly saw that some citizens might take pleasure from consuming more than their neighbors, but that might well have been at the heart of his mistake. Leijonhufvud claims that "a similar but somewhat less sordid incentive to consume is the desire to earn the respect of one's peers." As Frank argues, Keynes "seems to have believed that context mattered only for goods that 'lift us above,' or 'make us feel superior to, our fellows.' Like most other economists, he believed that demands originating in such feelings are at most a minor component of overall economic activity. I share that belief. Indeed few people are consciously aware of any desire to outdo their friends and neighbors. But the ways in which context shapes demand run far beyond such feelings ... [A] model [of the demand for quality] would be essentially identical to one based on a desire not to own quality for its own sake but rather to outdo, or avoid being outdone by, one's friends and neighbors. ... By placing the desire to outdo others at the heart of his description of the category of goods whose demands are shaped by context, Keynes confined that category to the periphery. The demand for quality is universal and inexhaustible."

Stiglitz points out that preferences might be endogenous. With advertisement and marketing-shaping preferences, individuals may be induced to value consumption (leisure) more and, even if wages do not increase, to work more (less) to satisfy their changing needs. This latter theory is useful as it would explain why certain societies seem to be shifting toward more and more leisure (Europe?) and others becoming more prone to consumerism (United States?).

Furthermore, increased inequality might have had an impact on consumption patterns. Leijonhufvud argues that tolerance for greater inequality in society might have increased due to greater income levels and the perception that basic needs are by now guaranteed. In turn, increased acceptance for inequality makes "relative needs" more accepted in society, as shown by the competition for status in the corporate world as well as in youth gangs.

Finally it should not be forgotten that Keynes was right at least in forecasting the vast decline in the saving rate of western economies. Frank claims that such a right prediction comes from wrong reasons, as declining saving have occurred with rising consumption levels. Perhaps, he argues, context here too has played a role: as income growth has been reserved to the top earners within each income group, the laggards might have felt left behind and might have reacted by consuming more of their income to keep up with their reference group.

Is this consumerism and addiction to work something to be worried about? Not all authors in the volume agree on this, as should be expected. Those who indeed express their worry argue that more publicly funded education (see Stiglitz and Zilibotti), redistribution (see Solow), or consumption taxation (see Frank) would bring about greater happiness, together with growth. The worry with these government policies, however, is that they might cause more troubles than advantages. After all, as Ohanian argues, in the aftermath of World War II "advanced economies were ultimately able to grow because the worst government policies of the 1920s and 1930s were reformed or eliminated."

Keynes on the Good Society

Economic Possibilities is more than a simple attempt at sketching out an economic fresco of the twenty-first century. It has the ambition of a philosophical treatise indicating an ideal society soon to come on earth.

Keynes believed that thanks to "purposeful money-makers" the world would achieve a state of economic abundance where people would be able to get rid of "pseudo-moral principles" (avarice, exaction of interest, love for money)—that have characterized capitalistic societies—and devote themselves to the true art of life. Capitalism—however detestable it might look—has the advantage that with its marvellous mechanism of compound interest it will take humankind toward the good society. This seems to be Keynes's only concession to capitalism. Fitoussi agrees with Keynes that economic progress should "serve moral objectives" but he disagrees with the caricatured picture Keynes offered of capitalism and its vices. For example, for Fitoussi it would be difficult to understand why *carpe diem* as a moral principle to guide our actions would be superior to the one—prevailing in a capitalistic society—that would give high consideration to the future. In the end the moral strength of capitalism is "its consequentialism as it can lead to intergenerational altruism."

The vision of the world of which we dream is the reflection of our personal experiences and cultural environments. In envisioning his ideal world Keynes is no exception. He had been at Eton and Cambridge and was an active member of the Bloomsbury Group, a literary group active in the field of art criticism and scholarship and also counting Virginia Woolf, Lytton Strachey, and E. M. Forster among its most prominent members. The Group rejected the Victorian and Edwardian restrictions on religious, social, and sexual issues. They promoted contemporary arts. They took anti-imperialistic and pacifistic positions in foreign policy, although these views were not always shared by Keynes. Robert Skidelsky says of Keynes's attachment to this group: "Bloomsbury was Keynes's conscience. . . . They were not just his friends but his ideal." The good society he had in mind was something arising from that cultural surrounding and experience. He was contemplating a sort of "elite communism," to use Fitoussi's pregnant definition. If we look at social customs, tastes, and at how people enjoy life in today's affluent societies, it is hard to find something that resembles the Bloomsbury lifestyle; at most it is a lifestyle reserved to a subset of the community. If anything, we observe a variety of lifestyles in today's customs. As Axel Leijonhufvud says: "People of Keynes's class and generation tended to think that economic progress would have to involve also the acculturation of the lower classes to bourgeois cultural values, and a variety of educational institutions were at one time founded to aid that process. Keynes, of course, was hoping to see bourgeois culture evolve away from what it then was in a Bloomsbury direction. But he would not have envisaged the middle classes emulating ghetto tastes."

Keynes was persuaded that "[W]hen the accumulation of capital is no longer of high social importance, there will be great changes in the moral code." In this Keynes was wrong and right at the same time. As many authors in this book emphasize, it is hard to believe that there will come a moment when people feel that the economic problem is solved and capital accumulation comes to an end. The aspiration for improvement is always there, no matter what level of living standard has been achieved, and with it the need to save, accumulate, and work. Keynes, however, was right in believing that rising living standards consist both of material and moral improvement.

This theme of socially responsive growth is extensively developed by Friedman who explicitly recognizes that people today live in "a more open, tolerant, fair and democratic society" thanks to the economic improvements that industrialized countries have achieved. However, he believes that the link between living standards and moral strength is fragile. The combination of economic stagnation and increasing inequality, which can be observed today in some high-income countries such as the United States and the United Kingdom, may impair the morality and the values of a good society. These recent developments especially in countries such as the United States and the United Kingdom made Friedman look at the future in a more gloomy way than Keynes did.

Becchetti takes a slightly different stand on these issues. He believes that a silent revolution or a "civil dissension" is actually taking place in an environment of global prosperity to correct some of the social imbalances that economic development is bringing about. According to Becchetti, in today's economies "the traditional system of checks and balances, which was typically performing the task of reconciling economic development with social justice in the past, is in a state of crisis." In the traditional system corporations were creating value and at the same time they were producing various negative externalities whose effects were mitigated by the action of powerful trade unions. Globalization has weakened this system. However, society has been able to produce endogenous defenses to contrast some of the undesired effects of the more competitive environment. According to Becchetti, the actions of concerned consumers and investors have compensated for the growing weakness of trade unions. The rising phenomenon of corporate social responsibility is the result of this bottom-up pressure. Data presented by Becchetti show that today one out of nine dollars under professional management in the United States is invested in socially responsible portfolios.

In the end many authors in this book tend to agree with Keynes that economic growth induces higher moral standards. Yet this relationship may be impaired by the existence of social imbalances or the excesses of a competitive environment. The transition to the good society or to higher levels of civilization appears to be a more complex and dialectical process than the one envisioned by Keynes.

Keynes's major contribution to economic theory at the time of writing *Economic Possibilities for our Grandchildren* had been the *Treatise on Money*, a lengthy work aimed at describing price dynamics in terms of discrepancies between planned saving and investment. No particular attention was paid to changes in the level of output and unemployment nor to effective demand, which would become the focus of his magnum opus *The General Theory*.

This makes it all the more remarkable that in the few pages of *Economic Possibilities* Keynes is sketching a primitive theory of technological unemployment and also a theory of effective demand failure.

Boldrin and Levine follow up this specific lead on technological unemployment, discarding, both on theoretical and empirical ground, the possibility that the reduction in employment in Britain in the 1930s could be the consequence of technological change leading to labor saving. In Keynes's defense, we can say that he must not have been fully convinced of this theory if he never mentioned it again in his successive writings. More promising is perhaps the sketched theory of effective demand.

Boldrin and Levine argue that Keynes implies that there are two sides in human attitude or, said in other terms, two types of human beings. The first type of people, including both workers and entrepreneurs, is the product of a long biological evolution that makes them prone to fall victim to the capitalistic ideology and to an unsuppressible need—to work and accumulate, even after reaching satiation. In this environment, demand tends to fall short of supply. The second type of people pursues the art of life and has abandoned the capitalistic ideology. At some point in the future the second type will prevail, everybody will work less, and unemployment will disappear. For those familiar with Keynes's writing it is not difficult to recognize here some primitive elements of the effective demand failure theory that will take its more complete form in *The General Theory*.

Several authors in this book, including Boldrin and Levine, find Keynes's tendency to take a moral high stand vis-à-vis capitalism when theorizing about human behavior disturbing.

First, Keynes's general disparagement of work is excessive to the point of snobbishness. Here is where his "Bloomsburyism" shows most. As Richard Freeman points out "many people go to work for reasons beyond money." Workplaces are social settings where people find a way to express themselves. This is true, of course, for high-level jobs but more and more so also for those jobs that are less prestigious.

Second, some authors are uncomfortable with Keynes's characterization of the "capitalistic ideal." One wonders if it is not misleading to put the love for money, or avarice, which is certainly a pathology existing in a capitalistic societies, at the center of the motives of human action, while plainly disregarding other important motives that may determine entrepreneurs' behavior. It is a pity that Keynes, when theorizing on these issues, turned to Sigmund Freud and ignored some insightful thoughts of his teacher Alfred Marshall, who claimed that: "The chemist or the physicist may happen to make money by his inventions, but that is seldom the chief motive of his work. . . . [B]usiness men are very much of the same nature as scientific men; they have the same instincts of the chase, and many of them have the same power of being stimulated to great and even feverish exertions by emulations that are not sordid or ignoble. This part of their nature has however been confused with and thrown into the shade by their desire to make money. . . . And so all the best business men want to get money, but many of them do not care about it much for its own sake; they want it chiefly as the most convincing proof to themselves and others that they have succeeded." (Pigou 1956, pp. 281–82)

Third, several authors in this book insist that Keynes failed to recognize the constant aspiration of humans to improve their condition as well as the satisfaction that may derive from exercising one's mind in facing new challenges. People are striving for knowledge, for exploring new things, for setting new goals, and not for a stagnant workless society. As Freeman eloquently put it: "Evolution presumably imbued us with a work ethic for our survival and not for a Garden of Eden existence." Similarly Phelps argues: "But if Keynes *had* recognized that people *need* a system that throws out problems to challenge the mind and engage the spirit, he would still have gone wrong. He never saw that with the technical progress and capital deepening that he aptly postulates, an ever-increasing share of people can afford jobs that are stimulating and engaging. So unless the economic system is prevented from doing so, more and more jobs will be supplied that offer stimulation and engagement."

Again, if Keynes had paid more attention to his old teacher, he could have probably changed some of his perspectives. Marshall developed the doctrine that it is new activities that give rise to new wants rather than the other way around. As people improve their conditions—moved both by the desire of excellence and distinction—they demand new and better things in an endless fashion. "It is, again, the desire for the exercise and development of activities, spreading through every rank of society, which leads not only to the pursuit of science, literature and art for their own sake, but to the rapidly increasing demand for the work of those who pursue them as professions. Leisure is used less and less as an opportunity for mere stagnation; and there is a growing desire for those amusements, such as athletic games and travelling, which develop activities rather than indulge any sensuous craving." (Marshall 1947, p. 88)

It is also surprising that Keynes, while theorizing about the achievement of a state of consumption satiation where humans would devote themselves to nothing else but the art of living, did not give any tribute to John Stuart Mill who developed a similar doctrine almost a century earlier. It is striking how the argument presented by Keynes in *Economic Possibilities* is close to the Mill's doctrine of the stationary state (Mill [1848] 1909, bk 4, ch. 6). Mill is convinced that the economic progress will come to an end and that at this end "lies the stationary state." However, he remarks that a stationary condition of capital and population does not imply a stationary state of human improvements, since "There would be as much scope as ever for all kinds of mental culture, and moral and social progress; as much room for improving the Art of Living, and much more likelihood of its being improved, when minds ceased to be engrossed by the art of getting on." Mill believed that in the stationary state people will improve their moral standing through a better distribution of property obtained by a system of legislation favoring "equality of fortunes" and against excessive concentration of property. He also believed that everyone has the right to a state of "solitude in the presence of natural beauty" that is "essential to any depth of meditation." In a world with continuous growing population nothing is left to the spontaneous activity of nature and the earth will "lose that great portion of its pleasantness."

After more than 150 years from Mill's meditations and 75 from those of Keynes, as the authors in this book remark, there are no signs that the world economy is moving toward a stationary state yet. Quite to the contrary, the capitalistic economy is spreading fast in all areas of the globe. Living standards are raising for millions of human beings. It also seems that people are willing to accept increasing levels of inequality as far as they can participate to this bonanza.

It is true that one of the undesired effects of economic growth is the emission of greenhouse gases that contribute to global warming. But in recent years we have witnessed a significant shift in the debate on climate change. Today it is no longer a theme restricted to scientists, it is part of daily discussion among citizens. In the business world firms are recasting their policies and their "corporate and social responsibility" claims, while governments are beginning to consider remedies. Even if such increased concern brings about some policies that have a negative effect on growth in the years to come, we do not need to take a gloomy view of the future. Again, the inventiveness of human beings can be expected to find good solutions to these problems through innovation and technical change.

We believe the reader will find much food for thought in the pages to follow. We are left with only one thing to say on Keynes and the century he lived in. Keynes did not predict the brutality that many of his grandchildren experienced during the twentieth century, from violent ideologies and infamous oppressions of free will, nations and religions. Maybe the twenty-first century that we leave to our grandchildren will be that of joyful work, endless innovations, and free entrepreneurship, all over the planet. This was not Keynes's favorite dream in 1930, but being a great thinker, he would probably agree with us today.

Bibliography

Harrod, F. R. 1972. *The Life of John Maynard Keynes*. London: Macmillan.

Keynes, J. M. 1935. *Economic Possibilities for our Grandchildren*. In J. M. Keynes, *Essays in Persuasion*. London: Macmillan.

Marshall, A. 1947. *Principles of Economics*. London: Macmillan.

Mill, J. S. [1848] 1909. *Principles of Political Economy with Some of Their Applications to Social Philosophy*. London: Logmans, Green.

Pigou, A. C. ed. 1956. *Memorials of Alfred Marshall*. New York: Kelley and Millman.

Skidelsky, R. 1992. *John Maynard Keynes: Volume 2: The Economist as Saviour*. London: Macmillan.

1   *Economic Possibilities for our Grandchildren* (1930)

John Maynard Keynes

I

We are suffering just now from a bad attack of economic pessimism. It is common to hear people say that the epoch of enormous economic progress which characterised the nineteenth century is over; that the rapid improvement in the standard of life is now going to slow down—at any rate in Great Britain; that a decline in prosperity is more likely than an improvement in the decade which lies ahead of us.

I believe that this is a wildly mistaken interpretation of what is happening to us. We are suffering, not from the rheumatics of old age, but from the growing-pains of over-rapid changes, from the painfulness of readjustment between one economic period and another. The increase of technical efficiency has been taking place faster than we can deal with the problem of labour absorption; the improvement in the standard of life has been a little too quick; the banking and monetary system of the world has been preventing the rate of interest from falling as fast as equilibrium requires. And even so, the waste and confusion which ensue relate to not more than $7\frac{1}{2}$ per cent of the national income; we are muddling away one and sixpence in the £, and have only 18s 6d, when we might, if we were more sensible, have £1; yet, nevertheless, the 18s 6d mounts up to as much as the £1 would have been five or six years ago. We forget that in 1929 the physical output of the industry of Great Britain was greater than ever before, and that the net surplus of our foreign balance available for new foreign investment, after paying for all our imports, was greater last year than that of any other country, being indeed 50 per cent greater than the corresponding surplus of the United States. Or again—if it is to be a matter

which Drake brought home in 1580 has now become £100,000. Such is
the power of compound interest!

From the sixteenth century, with a cumulative crescendo after the
eighteenth, the great age of science and technical inventions began,
which since the beginning of the nineteenth century has been in full
flood—coal, steam, electricity, petrol, steel, rubber, cotton, the chemi-
cal industries, automatic machinery and the methods of mass production, wireless, printing, Newton, Darwin, and Einstein, and thousands
of other things and men too famous and familiar to catalogue.

What is the result? In spite of an enormous growth in the population
of the world, which it has been necessary to equip with houses and
machines, the average standard of life in Europe and the United States
has been raised, I think, about fourfold. The growth of capital has been
on a scale which is far beyond a hundred-fold of what any previous
age had known. And from now on we need not expect so great an increase of population.

If capital increases, say, 2 per cent per annum, the capital equipment
of the world will have increased by a half in twenty years, and seven
and a half times in a hundred years. Think of this in terms of material
things—houses, transport, and the like.

At the same time technical improvements in manufacture and transport have been proceeding at a greater rate in the last ten years than
ever before in history. In the United States factory output per head
was 40 per cent greater in 1925 than in 1919. In Europe we are held
back by temporary obstacles, but even so it is safe to say that technical
efficiency is increasing by more than 1 per cent per annum compound.
There is evidence that the revolutionary technical changes, which have
so far chiefly affected industry, may soon be attacking agriculture. We
may be on the eve of improvements in the efficiency of food production as great as those which have already taken place in mining, manufacture, and transport. In quite a few years—in our own lifetimes I
mean—we may be able to perform all the operations of agriculture,
mining, and manufacture with a quarter of the human effort to which
we have been accustomed.

For the moment the very rapidity of these changes is hurting us and
bringing difficult problems to solve. Those countries are suffering relatively which are not in the vanguard of progress. We are being afflicted
with a new disease of which some readers may not yet have heard the
name, but of which they will hear a great deal in the years to come—
namely, *technological unemployment*. This means unemployment due to

our discovery of means of economising the use of labour outrunning the pace at which we can find new uses for labour.

But this is only a temporary phase of maladjustment. All this means in the long run *that mankind is solving its economic problem*. I would predict that the standard of life in progressive countries one hundred years hence will be between four and eight times as high as it is to-day. There would be nothing surprising in this even in the light of our present knowledge. It would not be foolish to contemplate the possibility of a far greater progress still.

II

Let us, for the sake of argument, suppose that a hundred years hence we are all of us, on the average, eight times better off in the economic sense than we are to-day. Assuredly there need be nothing here to surprise us.

Now it is true that the needs of human beings may seem to be insatiable. But they fall into two classes—those needs which are absolute in the sense that we feel them whatever the situation of our fellow human beings may be, and those which are relative in the sense that we feel them only if their satisfaction lifts us above, makes us feel superior to, our fellows. Needs of the second class, those which satisfy the desire for superiority, may indeed be insatiable; for the higher the general level, the higher still are they. But this is not so true of the absolute needs—a point may soon be reached, much sooner perhaps than we are all of us aware of, when these needs are satisfied in the sense that we prefer to devote our further energies to non-economic purposes.

Now for my conclusion, which you will find, I think, to become more and more startling to the imagination the longer you think about it.

I draw the conclusion that, assuming no important wars and no important increase in population, the *economic problem* may be solved, or be at least within sight of solution, within a hundred years. This means that the economic problem is not—if we look into the future—*the permanent problem of the human race*.

Why, you may ask, is this so startling? It is startling because—if, instead of looking into the future, we look into the past—we find that the economic problem, the struggle for subsistence, always has been hitherto the primary, most pressing problem of the human race—not only of the human race, but of the whole of the biological kingdom from the beginnings of life in its most primitive forms.

Thus we have been expressly evolved by nature—with all our impulses and deepest instincts—for the purpose of solving the economic problem. If the economic problem is solved, mankind will be deprived of its traditional purpose.

Will this be a benefit? If one believes at all in the real values of life, the prospect at least opens up the possibility of benefit. Yet I think with dread of the readjustment of the habits and instincts of the ordinary man, bred into him for countless generations, which he may be asked to discard within a few decades.

To use the language of to-day—must we not expect a general "nervous breakdown"? We already have a little experience of what I mean—a nervous breakdown of the sort which is already common enough in England and the United States amongst the wives of the well-to-do classes, unfortunate women, many of them, who have been deprived by their wealth of their traditional tasks and occupations— who cannot find it sufficiently amusing, when deprived of the spur of economic necessity, to cook and clean and mend, yet are quite unable to find anything more amusing.

To those who sweat for their daily bread leisure is a longed-for sweet—until they get it.

There is the traditional epitaph written for herself by the old charwoman:—

Don't mourn for me, friends, don't weep for me never,
For I'm going to do nothing for ever and ever.

This was her heaven. Like others who look forward to leisure, she conceived how nice it would be to spend her time listening-in-for there was another couplet which occurred in her poem:—

With psalms and sweet music the heavens'll be ringing,
But I shall have nothing to do with the singing.

Yet it will only be for those who have to do with the singing that life will be tolerable—and how few of us can sing!

Thus for the first time since his creation man will be faced with his real, his permanent problem—how to use his freedom from pressing economic cares, how to occupy the leisure, which science and compound interest will have won for him, to live wisely and agreeably and well.

The strenuous purposeful money-makers may carry all of us along with them into the lap of economic abundance. But it will be those peoples, who can keep alive, and cultivate into a fuller perfection, the art of life itself and do not sell themselves for the means of life, who will be able to enjoy the abundance when it comes.

Yet there is no country and no people, I think, who can look forward to the age of leisure and of abundance without a dread. For we have been trained too long to strive and not to enjoy. It is a fearful problem for the ordinary person, with no special talents, to occupy himself, especially if he no longer has roots in the soil or in custom or in the beloved conventions of a traditional society. To judge from the behaviour and the achievements of the wealthy classes to-day in any quarter of the world, the outlook is very depressing! For these are, so to speak, our advance guard—those who are spying out the promised land for the rest of us and pitching their camp there. For they have most of them failed disastrously, so it seems to me—those who have an independent income but no associations or duties or ties—to solve the problem which has been set them.

I feel sure that with a little more experience we shall use the new-found bounty of nature quite differently from the way in which the rich use it to-day, and will map out for ourselves a plan of life quite otherwise than theirs.

For many ages to come the old Adam will be so strong in us that everybody will need to do *some* work if he is to be contented. We shall do more things for ourselves than is usual with the rich to-day, only too glad to have small duties and tasks and routines. But beyond this, we shall endeavour to spread the bread thin on the butter—to make what work there is still to be done to be as widely shared as possible. Three-hour shifts or a fifteen-hour week may put off the problem for a great while. For three hours a day is quite enough to satisfy the old Adam in most of us!

There are changes in other spheres too which we must expect to come. When the accumulation of wealth is no longer of high social importance, there will be great changes in the code of morals. We shall be able to rid ourselves of many of the pseudo-moral principles which have hag-ridden us for two hundred years, by which we have exalted some of the most distasteful of human qualities into the position of the highest virtues. We shall be able to afford to dare to assess the money-motive at its true value. The love of money as a possession—as distinguished from the love of money as a means to the enjoyments margin between our production and our consumption; of which the last will easily look after itself, given the first three.

Meanwhile there will be no harm in making mild preparations for our destiny, in encouraging, and experimenting in, the arts of life as well as the activities of purpose.

But, chiefly, do not let us overestimate the importance of the economic problem, or sacrifice to its supposed necessities other matters of greater and more permanent significance. It should be a matter for specialists—like dentistry. If economists could manage to get themselves thought of as humble, competent people, on a level with dentists, that would be splendid!

2 Economic Possibilities for our Grandchildren 75 Years After: A Global Perspective

Fabrizio Zilibotti

In the heart of the Great Crisis, amid great uncertainty and concerns surrounding the future of capitalism, John Maynard Keynes launched his optimistic prophecy that growth and technological change will allow humankind to *solve its economic problem* within a century. He envisioned a world where people work much less and are less oppressed by the satisfaction of material needs. He made quantitative statements predicting that "the standard of life in progressive countries one hundred years hence will be between four and eight times as high..." as in his time. And he wrote about work time that "...a fifteen-hour week may put off the problem for a great while." He also expected the new era to bring about "great changes in the code of morals," such that the new society will "honour those who can teach (us) how to pluck the hour and the day virtuously and well, the delightful people who are capable of taking direct enjoyment in things...."

To what extent have his predictions turned out to be accurate? Economic growth indeed resumed during the 1930s, but the conflagration of World War II was soon to come. Yet the engine of growth restarted at the end of the war, and the world thereafter underwent an unprecedented transformation. And people today indeed spend a smaller fraction of their lives in work activity. However, there are large differences in both standards of living and attitudes toward work across countries and individuals.

A Half-century of Growth: The Empirical Evidence

I will begin by diverging from Keynes's focus on "progressive countries" and considering the long-run growth experience of the entire global economy. Version 6.1 of the Penn World Tables provides a panel of annual observations for 168 countries during the period 1950

Fabrizio Zilibotti

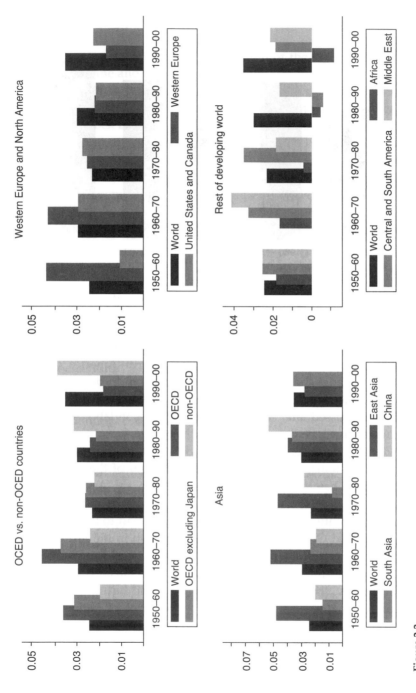

Figure 2.2
Regional growth rates from 1950 to 2000.

the half-century was low, and the trend even more discouraging in the 1980s and 1990s when the standards of living fell rather than improving. By 2000 the average GDP per capita of sub-Saharan African countries was US$1,576, slightly exceeding a mere 6 percent of the average GDP per capita in OECD economies. It will take a century of steady 3 percent annual growth for the average sub-Saharan African country to attain the standards of living rich countries enjoy today.

In summary, humankind has managed to attain, on average, major progress in the second half of the twentieth century, well beyond Keynes's optimistic expectations. Nevertheless, the solution of the economic problem is still distant for a large share of the world. By 2000, the average GDP per capita among non-OECD countries (which represent more vast majority of the world population) was still short of the GDP per capita of the United States a century earlier. The tragedy of sub-Saharan Africa remains as acute as ever, with AIDS, civil wars, and political unrest making miserable living conditions for the majority of its 600 million inhabitants. There are further unpleasant developments: within-country inequality has increased all over the world, making the increase of extreme poverty in the low-performing regions even more dramatic.[7]

Why do standards of living persistently remain so diverse? Part of the difference is due to capital accumulation. But, as a number of recent studies document, an even larger part is due technological differences (or differences in "total factor productivity"). Poor countries fail to adopt the more productive technologies that firms use in the industrialized world, or only do so with a significant delay. Explaining why the diffusion of ideas and technical improvements remains so slow worldwide is the subject of a long-standing debate. Institutional and political failures generating barriers to technology adoption are certainly an important factor.[8] In Acemoglu and Zilibotti (2001) we argue that even if such barriers were absent, the process of innovation originating in the industrialized world may produce technologies which are "inappropriate" for the needs of the developing world, because of the complementarity of new technologies with human skills. Innovations in developed countries tend to evolve new technologies that require skilled workers (*vide* the IT revolution in the 1990s). The scarcity of highly educated workers limits the ability of poor economies to benefit from these technologies, inhibiting technological convergence.[9] The concurrent presence of growth-promoting institutions and high educational investment indeed seems to be the key of the success in South and East Asian economies.

More Income or More Leisure?

Keynes forecasted that a consequence of the material progress would be a reduction in the time people devote to working activities. He posited that because consumption needs would be subject to some satiation, every person would only need to work about fifteen hours a week.

A strong trend toward the reduction of the work time was recorded well before Keynes's forecast (see Marimon and Zilibotti 2000). According to the estimates reported by Huberman and Minns (2005), the average annual number of hours worked per worker fell by almost 30 percent between 1870 and 1930, in both Europe and the United States. The sharpest drop actually occurred in the three first decades of the twentieth century, so the trend must have made a strong impression on Keynes's contemporaries. After World War II, on the one hand, the number of hours per worker fell further, but at a lower rate, and more in Europe than in the United States. On the other hand, the female labor participation increased significantly, partially offsetting the decline in the number of hours worked by male workers. To date, the working week has not fallen to fifteen hours anywhere in the world, nor can we reasonably expect this to occur by the year 2030. A number of factors should, however, be taken into consideration in order to assess how much leisure people enjoy today.

First, work time as a share of an individual's life has indeed fallen significantly. By 2000, life expectancy in Great Britain was about twenty years longer than it was in 1930 (seventeen in the United States). Although part of this difference can be attributed to lower infant mortality, life expectancy is also significantly higher, rising for the US white males at age twenty by approximately ten years, and the even higher for females and ethnic minority groups. Likewise the life expectancy of white males aged sixty also rose from fifteen to twenty years in the same period. In contrast, retirement age fell. The median retirement age for men in the United States has fallen, again by 2000, from age seventy to age sixty-two (see Eisensee 2006). This means that the fraction of an individual's lifetime spent on working activities is much smaller today than in 1930.

Let us construct a fictitious "Keynes forecast." Suppose that Keynes did not anticipate the changes in life expectancy, female participation rate, and retirement age. In this scenario, an agent who enters the labor force at fifteen works fifteen hours per week with probability 60 percent up to age sixty-five, then works fifteen hours with probability 30 percent up to age seventy, and then dies. Here, age seventy matches the life expectancy of a twenty-year-old in 1930, while 60 and 30 percent are the share of employed people in the respective age group.[10] Now contrast "Keynes's forecast" with a 2000 real world scenario, where an agent enters the labor force when fifteen, then works (in two alternative experiments matching, broadly the European and US experience) either thirty or thirty-eight hours per week with probability 70 percent up to age sixty-five, then lives as a retiree up to age eighty, and then dies.[11] In both cases assume agents to have at their disposal sixteen hours a day (with eight hours being devoted to sleeping), and I ignore the lifetime between birth and age fifteen.

The results are as follows: In Keynes's forecast, the average individual works 7.6 percent of her/his lifetime endowment. In contrast, in my 2000 real world analysis, she/he works 14.4 percent of her/his lifetime in the thirty hours workweek case, and 18.3 percent in the thirty-eight hours workweek case.

Second, Keynes expected affluence to free time for leisure. If we want to know how much time people can devote to enjoyment, we must subtract from the time available to humans not only the number of hours they work in the market but also the time they spend in house-related work activity. I should stress up front that there is no consensus in the literature about the secular trend in housework. According to the estimates reported by Greenwood et al. (2005), housework per US household amounted to an average forty hours in 1930. A recent study by Achen and Stafford (2005) based on the Panel of Study of Income Dynamics (PSID) concludes that in 2001 this amounted (for married couples in the United States) to 25 hours per week. Assuming that the data are comparable, more than one hour per person per day was freed from the yoke of housework. Such change has been made possible by labor-saving technical improvements in basic facilities and electrical appliances (running water, refrigerator, washer, vacuum, etc.). Not all the time saved at home has been devoted to leisure, though, and the study of Greenwood et al. (2005) attributes an increase of about 28 percent points in the female labor supply between 1900 and 1980 to the technological revolution in the household sector.[12]

Third, people spend today a larger share of their time on educational activities. Ramey and Francis (2006) report that the annual per capita hours in a cross section of the US population spent on school rose from six hundred to nine hundred in the period 1970 to 2000. How should we regard this pursuit of learning? I suspect that Keynes would count it as one of the benefits of humankind's liberation from the necessity of material production. But if one takes the pessimistic view that educational effort is as painful as working in a mine, one may want to account the increase in education as an offsetting factor in the secular reduction of worktime.

Because people work for a smaller fraction of their lives today than in 1930, I believe they do enjoy more leisure, although I acknowledge that there is not overwhelming consensus on this point. Technological progress has had equally important effects on the quality of work time and leisure activities. Working conditions are better and more pleasing. And if, to put it like Keynes, "three hours a day is quite enough to satisfy the old Adam in most of us," entering the labor market had some positive implications for Eve. Labor participation and the possibility of developing a career have been vehicles of female emancipation. Finally, technical progress has increased the variety of leisure goods and reduced the time necessary for performing many leisure activities (e.g., progress in transportation facilities makes it possible to travel more extensively and in a shorter time).

I would like also to comment on the adaptability of labor supply over the last thirty years to technological progress, and the different tastes developed by European and Americans on how to enjoy the fruits of this progress. Europeans have extended—perhaps following Keynes's inclination—their leisure hours, while Americans have chosen longer work hours. More precisely, back in the mid-1970s Britons, Germans, and Frenchmen worked on average 5 to 10 percent more than Americans. At the turn of this century, however, they work only 70 to 75 percent of their American counterparts (see Prescott 2004, tab. 1).[13] Interestingly, although the GDP per capita grew faster in the United States than in Europe, the opposite occurred with output per hour worked. The GDP per hour increased by 38 percent in the United States between 1970 and 2000, while the GDP per hour in France rose by 83 percent in the same period.[14] Germany and other continental European countries behaved much like France. This is almost entirely due to the labor supply behavior. What can explain this difference? According to Prescott (2004), the key is cross-country differences in the distortionary effects of labor income tax. Blanchard (2004) attributes this difference to Europeans choosing a more balanced allocation of the productivity gains between increasing income and leisure. Whether as a matter of taste or as the effect of policies (which are in any case the outcome of democratic processes), Europeans seem to be moving in the direction Keynes suggested. Whether movement in this direction will be steady is uncertain, however, especially since the demographic trend of increasing retirees in the population and work time reductions among the active population such that may jeopardize the sustainability of the pension system.

Why do Americans work more hours than forecasted by Keynes? Economic theory offers no compelling reason for technological progress that impells people to work less. Textbook economics teach us that as productivity grows, income and substitution effects work in opposite directions: as we get richer, we demand more leisure (income effect), but at the same time we become more conscious of the increase in its opportunity cost (substitution effect). With standard preferences, the net effect can go either way.

Nevertheless, Keynes proposed a sophisticated argument that goes beyond the simple trade-off between labor and leisure. By his argument, some evolutionary process (or learning) affects the intensity with which people are capable of enjoying leisure or tolerating labor effort. The ability to appreciate leisure would depend on some acquired taste and, possibly, on complementary investments increasing the ability to appreciate specific leisure activities. For instance, it takes time, effort, and devotion to appreciate literature or classical music. In Keynes's view, the secular slavery of economic necessity has selected human preferences for a high tolerance of labor effort and some limited ability to appreciate good life. Keynes anticipated that the progressive satiation of material needs would naturally generate a shift of preferences, whereby people would become better at appreciating arts and beauty. Moral values would also change, and the obsession for money-making would be replaced by a new humanism.

Interestingly the recent economic literature on "endogenous preferences" echoes this view. For instance, we use a similar—if somewhat opposite—argument in Doepke and Zilibotti (2005, 2008) to explain the decline of the aristocratic elite at the outset of the British industrial revolution. We argue that the pre-industrial elite, accustomed as it was to rearing its children in the devotion to arts, pleasures, and a variety of leisure-oriented activities (from classical music to fox hunting), developed a sense of disdain for hard work and a low propensity to save and invest. The urban middle class, in contrast, was reared in the values of thriftiness and perseverance which were most important in the life experience of artisans and traders. For this reason, the latter developed a "capitalist spirit" that, as emphasized in the celebrated work of Max Weber, became a major advantage once new opportunities arose with the Industrial Revolution. This can explain the triumph of the bourgeoisie and the demise of the aristocracy during the Industrial Revolution.

Keynes's argument goes one step further in time. He argues that when economic needs are satiated, a reversal will occur, and the appreciation of arts and leisure will again become the evolutionary successful trait. Can we see evidence of the change predicted by Keynes? Hardly, in my view. The growing phenomenon of obesity is emblematic of the quantitative (as opposed to qualitative) nature of people's consumption habits. Another is the growing pressure for downsizing the provision of public goods such as health services, green areas, or elderly care that affect people's daily quality of life. The return to these savings is yet more private consumption, in a society where private opulence risks being coupled with public poverty. Markets seem to have been proved capable of supplying an amazing quantity and variety of leisure goods that require more money than time to be enjoyed. These goods are strong competitors for traditional cultural consumption goods, requiring lengthy training and education toward their appreciation. But the last word has not been said, and we may just be learning to appreciate the good life too slowly.

Conclusion

Did Keynes's optimism prove warranted? His expectations about improvements in the material conditions of mankind were correct. Material progress has indeed led to extraordinary expansion of the opportunities that we can today enjoy. Keynes's forecasts about the cultural implications of growth are more problematic, and material needs do not show any clear tendency of becoming satiated.

Material progress continues, however, to be the primary problem for large parts of the world, especially for the 600 million people who continue to live in conditions of extreme poverty. My hope is that growth will be contagious and spread in the developing world. Although future generations may decide to enjoy the fruit of the technological progress in different ways, including shorter work time, I do not expect productivity growth and technological change to slow down in industrialized economies.

Nevertheless, growth is not just about good news. I see environmental sustainability as a major unresolved question. I cannot subscribe to the optimism of many economists in this respect. There are neither effective self-correcting nor, to date, institutional mechanisms that can prevent a "tragedy of the commons" on a global scale. We can hope that technological progress will move more in the natural resource-saving direction. But this will not come through the invisible hand. It will instead hinge on a strong political will to constrain and make more expensive the use and abuse of natural resources as well as the emission of pollutants. On the one hand, the action of special interest groups in some rich countries is blocking these necessary interventions; on the other hand, environmental issues remain a luxury good for countries striving to solve their "economic problem." If these countries decide to use natural resources as intensively as the first industrializers, the environmental effects might be dramatic. The only hope for success is for rich countries to induce poorer countries, through their financial and technical support and via incentive-compatible mechanisms, to adopt environmentally friendly technologies. The set of current international institutions is far too underdeveloped to tackle this issue. The risk of a global failure is, in my view, severe.

Notes

I thank Gino Gancia, Sally Gschwend, Dirk Niepelt, and Maria Saez Marti for very useful comments.

1. The dataset is available online at *http:/pwt.econ.upenn.edu/php_site/ pwt_index.php.*

2. Since China accounts for almost one-fourth of the world population, not having China in the dataset before 1952, but having it thereafter, would affect significantly the estimate of the world average growth rate. In my estimates China is always included.

3. More precisely, the annual growth rate of the world (or of any subset of it) is the arithmetic average of the growth rates of all countries in the sample, where each observation is weighted by its population size (e.g., in year 2000, China has a weight of 0.24 while Switzerland has a weight of 0.0014). The five-year average is then constructed as an average of the relevant five annual observations.

4. By construction, population-weighted average growth rates differ from the growth rate of the average GDP per capita in the world. For example, suppose that the world consists of two countries with identical populations, A and B. Let A and B have, respectively, a GDP of 100 and 200. Suppose that the GDP doubles in A and remains constant in B (thus the world GDP increases from 300 to 400). Then the population-weighted average growth rate is 50 percent, whereas the world average GDP only grows 33 percent. The latter measure understates, relative to the one I use, the performance of low-income countries.

My measure provides, conceptually, an answer the following question: What is the annual growth rate in an individual's standards of living, if she or he, behind the veil of ignorance, is dropped in a random country in 1950? Interestingly, if one focuses on the alternative measure, the growth rate is 2.2 percent, which matches Keynes's forecast very closely.

5. I regard Korea and Mexico as non-OECD countries as they only entered the organization in 1994 and 1996, respectively. The results are shown both with and without the inclusion of Japan, since Japan is a large country that was relatively poor in 1950 and had an exceptionally strong performance.

6. The data for India are presented here jointly with Bangladesh, Bhutan, Nepal, Pakistan, and Sri Lanka. Although none of these countries performed as strongly as India, the average regional performance is only marginally affected, as India is by far the largest country.

7. For instance, Sala-i-Martin (2006) estimates that the number of people living with less than one and a half USD per day in Africa has increased by more than 200 million between 1970 and 2000.

8. See, for example, Parente and Prescott (2002) and Acemoglu et al. (2006).

9. In Acemoglu and Zilibotti (2001), we calibrate a growth model with endogenous technical change where the extent to which new technologies enhance the productivity of skilled and unskilled workers is also endogenous. The model can account for a large share of the empirical variation in cross-country total factor productivity differences.

10. In 2000, the employment rate (i.e., the proportion of employed in the population aged 15–64) was about 70 percent in the Anglo-Saxon world (65 percent in the average OECD). As stated in the text, I construct the "pseudo-Keynes forecast" by ignoring the increase in the female participation rate and other changes in labor supply behavior. In 1930, the female participation rates in the United States and United Kingdom were, respectively, 26 and 35 percent, whereas they amounted to 60 and 53 percent, respectively, in 2000 (see Costa 2000). Since changes in the length of education and early retirement went in the opposite direction, I assume that Keynes underestimated the actual employment rate by 10 percent points (60 percent in the "Keynes forecast" vs. 70 percent in the "2000 real world").

In addition many elderly were working before the establishment of modern pension systems (e.g., about 40 percent of males above 65 were working in major OECD countries in 1950). For this reason I assume in the "Keynes forecast" that 30 percent of the population over 65 is at work. In contrast, no retiree is assumed to work in the "2000 real world."

I should also stress that my simple calculation assumes, for simplicity, a constant population age structure. See Ramey and Francis (2006) for a thorough discussion.

11. European employed workers (both full- and part-time) worked in 2000 an average 30 to 33 hours a week, and enjoy roughly 35 days of holidays and vacation. In the United States, the corresponding figure is 38 hours, and with roughly 20 days of holidays and vacation.

12. Ramey and Francis (2006) criticize the data of Greenwood et al. (2005). According to their evidence, housework per capita, somewhat surprisingly, did not fall, and even increased in the United States in the period 1900 to 2000. Their study reports that housewives did over 50 hours housework a week around 1930s (see p. 16 and fig. 8). This is double the housework done by American couples in the PSID in 2001, according to the study of Achen and Stafford (2005).

13. The data in the text, borrowed from Prescott's study, detail hours worked per person aged 15 to 64. Thus they include persons who are unemployed or out of the labor force. If instead we look at weekly hours per worker in 2000, they were 38 in the United States, 33 in the United Kingdom, and between 30 and 32 in continental Europe.

14. The example and figures are from Blanchard (2004).

Bibliography

Acemoglu, D., P. Aghion, and F. Zilibotti. 2006. Distance to frontier, Selection and economic growth. *Journal of the European Economic Association* 4: 37–74.

Acemoglu, D., and F. Zilibotti. 2001. Productivity differences. *Quarterly Journal of Economics* 116: 536–606.

Achen, A. C., and F. P. Stafford. 2005. Data quality of housework hours in the panel study of income dynamics: Who really does the dishes? Mimeo. University of Michigan.

Blanchard, O. J. 2004. Is Europe falling behind. *The Globalist*, June 8.

Costa, Dora. 2000. From mill town to board room: The rise of women's paid labor. *Journal of Economic Perspectives* 14 (Fall): 101–22.

Doepke, M., and F. Zilibotti. 2005. Social class and the spirit of capitalism. *Journal of the European Economic Association* 3: 516–24.

Doepke, M., and F. Zilibotti. 2008. Occupational choice and the spirit of capitalism. *Quarterly Journal of Economics*, forthcoming.

Eisensee, T. 2006. Fiscal policy and retirement in the twentieth century. Mimeo. IIES-Stockholm University.

Greenwood, J., A. Seshadri, and M. Yourukoglu. 2005. Engines of liberation. *Review of Economic Studies* 72: 109–33.

Huberman, M., and C. Minns. 2007. The times they are not changin': Days and hours of work in old and new worlds, 1870–2000. In *Explorations in Economic History*, forthcoming.

Marimon, R., and F. Zilibotti. 2000. Employment and distributional effects of restricting working time. *European Economic Review* 44: 1291–1326.

Myrdal, G. 1968. *Asian Drama: An Inquiry into the Poverty of Nations.* New York: Pantheon Books.

Parente, S., and E. Prescott. 2002. *Barriers to Riches.* Cambridge: MIT Press.

Prescott, E. 2004. Why do Americans work so much more than Europeans. *Federal Reserve Bank of Minneapolis Quarterly Review* 28: 2–14.

Ramey, V., and N. Francis. 2006. A century of work and leisure. NBER working paper W12264.

Sala-i-Martin, X. 2006. The world distribution of income: Falling poverty and . . . convergence, period. *Quarterly Journal of Economics* 121: 351–97.

3 Toward a General Theory of Consumerism: Reflections on Keynes's *Economic Possibilities for our Grandchildren*

Joseph E. Stiglitz

Keynes's *Economic Possibilities for our Grandchildren* is as fascinating for the hidden assumptions about the nature of man as it for the predictions—clearly wrong—about the evolution of the economy. Keynes suggests that because of the huge improvements in technological possibilities and accumulation of capital, the *economic problem*— providing the necessities of life—will be solved, opening up a new world, in which each of us could devote our energies to higher callings. He suggests moreover that many of the conventions and institutions of society have arisen to solve the economic problem; shorn of those needs, a whole new set of institutions and social conventions may arise.

Keynes underestimated, by an order of magnitude, the pace of innovation as well as the rate at which capital could be accumulated—and invested well. The world had never seen anything like China, with its saving rate in excess of 40 percent and with growth rates averaging 9.7 percent for three decades. Even the more modest global growth rates of 3 to 4 percent that emerged in the years after World War II and persisted through the early 1970s, and which once again occurred, at least in the United States, beginning in the early 1990s, were unprecedented. Had Keynes been right about what such increases in output per capita portended, it is clear that the new world he envisioned would already be on the horizon.

The *possibility* of solving the economic problem (as he called it) is, of course, already on hand. If the more than $48 trillion dollar global GDP[1] were divided equally among the earth's some six and a half billion inhabitants, each would have some $7,000, more than enough to bring everyone out of poverty. (That number is even greater than America's poverty line for a family of 4.[2]) The key issue—to which Keynes repeatedly paid insufficient attention—is that of distribution.

While most of those in the advanced industrial countries have more than enough to meet their economic needs, some 50 percent of the world still lives on less than two dollars a day, some one billion still live on less than a dollar a day.[3] These individuals confront the economic problem of subsistence day in and day out; our society has failed to provide an answer for them.

How has the rest of the world confronted the challenge of the elimination of "the economic problem"? It is clear that the fundamental changes that Keynes seems to have predicted have not occurred. To be sure, institutions and practices have changed; for instance, Keynesian economics itself has led to a major shift in the conduct of macroeconomic policy. But the evolutionary changes that have occurred do not relate to the "solution" of the economic problem; rather, they have focused on how we can produce more goods more efficiently and how we can deliver them more efficiently. The underlying economic "model" has remained essentially unchanged.[4]

What Is to Be Explained?

If individuals don't "need" the income that they earn to meet their basic economic needs, what will people do with their *potential* leisure? Keynes strikes a pessimistic note, as he refers to those who have been relieved of economic burdens, "the wives of the well-to-do classes, unfortunate women...who [have been] quite unable to find anything more amusing." He did not, of course, anticipate the advent of television, which manages to absorb a huge chunk of the waking hours of both those who are gainfully employed and those who are not.[5]

The puzzle suggested by Keynes's paper, though, is not so much what people have done with their leisure, but why they have chosen to enjoy so little leisure. Why do people work as hard and as long as they do? Why have increased wages and wealth translated mostly into increased goods, not into increased leisure? Keynes seems to have overestimated the desire for leisure, especially in the United States, where people appear to be working about the same number of hours as thirty years ago: average weekly hours worked by persons of working age in the United States went from 24 in 1970 to 25 in 2004.[6] A particular aspect of this puzzle is the growing differences in leisure within the advanced industrial countries (e.g., between the United States and Sweden). While it is hard to get fully comparable data, it appears that

Americans work far more hours than do comparable individuals in other countries at similar levels of development. Especially striking are the changes that have occurred over the last third of a century. In 1970, there was little difference between the United States and France or Germany or the United Kingdom; by 2000, Americans were working some 40 percent more than the French, Italians or Belgians.[7]

Not only do Europeans work less today than Americans, but they also vacation more. The French take an average of seven weeks of vacation a year (including holidays) while the Germans take close to eight. The average in the United States is four weeks.[8]

Is it possible that a society could go down a path of "excess consumerism"? Is it possible that, of two societies, initially similar, one ends up consuming more, the other less? In this chapter, I argue that at, best, the standard model of consumer behavior provides little insight into these fundamental questions; at worst, what it says about the efficiency of free market outcomes is misleading. I say *fundamental* because there are few issues of more import than how society responds to the opportunities that improvements of technology have afforded. America, as a whole, has responded in ways that seem to have made less of a difference to the lives of the vast majority of its citizens than Keynes suggested; solving the economic problem simply hasn't made that much of a difference. In some ways, as I suggest, individuals and families may even be worse off. Problems of epidemic levels of obesity and of individuals working so hard to get what they view as the basics of life for their families *that they have no time to spend with their families* suggests dysfunctional behavior. If Galbraith could write about excessive consumption in 1958 in *Affluent Society*,[9] what would he say about America today? As much as economists may be loath to form judgments—are people really consuming more and enjoying leisure less than they *should*?—it is hard not to entertain the possibility that something is wrong, that there is something here to be explained.

In some of the simpler models we explore here, there are clear market failures where government interventions—such as mandatory vacations—would lead to Pareto improvements.

But even more strongly, once we open up the possibility that preferences are endogenous, there is no presumption that private market solutions have any optimality properties. By the same token, while the kinds of policy prescriptions, calling for government interventions, that arise naturally from our analysis may not be as theoretically tight

it does not recognize the enjoyment of work (whether in the market or at home). The standard model views work as a "cost," yet work gives meaning to life for many individuals. The distinction is at best blurred. For a farmer to toil in his fields is work, but for a middle-class American or European to toil in his garden is pleasure. Cooking may be toil, but for many individuals—and for almost all individuals on occasion—cooking is a pleasure. Similarly, commuting to work (which would presumably normally be added to market hours worked) may entail some elements of leisure (if individuals can read for pleasure), but the nature may change over time (as individuals conduct business over the cell phone or as crowded trains make commuting less pleasurable). As a result I have not attached much weight to the studies emphasizing that because the number of hours of home work has been reduced, true leisure has increased. (In addition this finding cannot explain the differences between the United States and Europe, since the same changes in the technologies of home production have occurred in both regions.)

Is writing this chapter toil or leisure? There is no direct financial return. I do it because thinking about these ideas gives me pleasure. Thinking about the puzzles—and trying to articulate the answers in ways that are clear to others—is hard work; yet doing so gives me enormous pleasure, which clearly exceeds the "work," for otherwise I would not be doing this.

Even in jobs that are themselves not very fulfilling, there can be considerable pleasure in the social interactions that occur at work. And even when individuals are sitting at their desks, they may be playing a game of solitaire on their computer, pleasurably daydreaming, or talking with friends on the phone. Difficult to observe, and even more difficult to quantify, changes in the nature of these pleasurable aspects of work—and differences between these aspects of work in Europe and the United States—could partially account for observed patterns of hours spent at work.[11]

If jobs were easily divisible, this observation would have little consequence: individuals would work to the point where work turned from a marginal benefit to a marginal cost, and the usual calculus would apply. The fact that individuals enjoy work would mean, of course, that as wages increase, the amount of time spent working might not decrease, even if consumption itself was subject to rapidly diminishing marginal utility. Labor supply will not diminish below the critical level where the marginal disutility of work is zero, and as labor approaches that critical level, changes in wages may have an increasingly small impact on leisure.

If, however, there are indivisibilities in work (increasing returns to scale)—it is difficult, for instance, for the job of CEO to be divided between two individuals—then, in competitive markets, individuals may, in effect, bid for jobs, and the winning bid may entail low levels of leisure. As productivity increases, the winning bids may, however, entail little changes in hours; indeed, if the costs of coordination increase as the complexity of the economy increases, the winning bid may actually involve more hours, with an offsetting increase in compensation.

This analysis helps explain why we might not expect *measured* leisure to increase, even as technologies improve, but it has a further import: it will be difficult to measure true leisure. Given the pleasures associated with work—both at home and in the "market"—the distinction between work and pleasure is not always well defined. Yet for many workers in our economy—those whose jobs are marked by drudgery or backbreaking physical exertion—it is not the enjoyment of work that drives them to work every day, and, for these, the puzzle is still there: Why are so many Americans working so long and so hard?

There is another explanation for why the demand for leisure may not have increased in the way that Keynes seems to have anticipated: wages, at least in the United States, *for most workers*, have not in fact increased. Median wages for American males in their thirties (a good predictor of lifetime incomes) were indeed lower in 2004 than they were in 1974.[12] Higher real wages might have led to more leisure; the problem, however, was that for most workers, real wages simply were not increasing. More generally, aggregate (average) levels of leisure depend on the distribution of income/wealth. Economic theory has no clear prediction on whether an increase in dispersion—such as the United States has experienced in the last third of a century—can lead to an increase or decrease in average (aggregate) leisure.[13]

Finally, demand for leisure may not have increased as Keynes predicted because labor force participation decisions are affected by social mores, and changes in social mores occur differently in different countries. One of the large differences (between the United States today and thirty years ago) is in female labor force participation.[14] It has become the norm for women to participate in the labor force, which is evidence of increased gender equality. Lowering of barriers to women working would be expected to lead to more labor force participation. This may be true even more so if there is pleasure in work, at least up to some level. In this view, we should be celebrating the increase in hours worked by women. There is, however, one telling criticism of this euphoric interpretation: lowering of the barriers could be viewed as a further increase in household productivity, an outward movement in their opportunity set, one that would normally be expected to lead to more consumption of leisure by the household, not less consumption. (In any case, differences in female labor force participation do not explain differences between the United States and Europe.[15])

There Is Something to Be Explained

The arguments in the preceding paragraphs have explained why it is possible to reconcile the failure for leisure to increase as much as Keynes's analysis would have suggested with standard economic theory. As is so often the case, standard theory seems to suggest that *anything is possible*. In that sense it has little predictive power. Keynes can be thought of as putting forth particular hypotheses concerning the shapes of preference functions; what is clear is that the observed behavior seems inconsistent with these hypotheses. We have, evidently, *not* solved the economic problem. Human desire for material goods is clearly insatiable. To be sure, one can only eat so many calories but can consume calories that are more expensive (e.g., meat vs. vegetables), and may get increased enjoyment out of these more expensive calories than out of the less expensive calories.

There is, however, still something to be explained. Increased wages might lead individuals to work a little more (or, as Keynes suggested, much less), but it does not seem plausible that it would lead them to work so much more that the quality of their life suffers. Yet leisure has diminished to the point that we are developing a "harried working class," with both parents working so hard—supposedly to enhance the quality of life with their families—that they have no time to share with their families.[16] While data on "happiness" remain controversial, studies suggest that the increased productivity in America's economy has not resulted in greater happiness.[17]

Equally troubling are the seeming trade-offs that Americans are making: they often seem to work hard for goods of which the value is hard to ascertain. Like perhaps other parts of Americans' needs—such as the need of even city dwellers to have SUV vehicles, four-wheel-drive cars designed for off-road traveling—these are just made-up needs, to compensate for the disappearance of real economic needs, part of America's approach to dealing with "solving the economic problem."

The statistics suggesting very high real incomes may indeed themselves be somewhat misleading. I wrote earlier about the great strides in efficiency—efficiency in production. But efficiency in production need not correspond to *systemic* efficiency, nor efficiency in consumption. Building superhighways that encourage individuals to travel long distances to work, in turn emitting high levels of pollution, may not represent a "systemically" efficient system of residential location cum production. Solving efficiently these systemic problems is enormously difficult. When we do not solve them efficiently—and markets typically do not—then increases in measured GDP per capita may grossly overstate increases in standards of living.

One aspect of America's pattern of living that may be associated with less efficient production of true consumption goods may be related to the deterioration in communal life.[18] Mothers used to play a more active role in their children's schools, enhancing the quality of these and other *public* or *communal* goods. As women have increasingly joined the labor force, such participation has declined, with a resulting decline in the quality of public schools.[19] Parents as a result compensate by spending more on private education (as a substitute or complement of public schools), but this increases their demand for income. A vicious circle is created—there may be multiple equilibria, one with high communal participation and lower labor force participation and one with lower communal participation and higher labor force participation. The level of well-being may be higher in the former, though the *measured* GDP would be higher in the latter.

A considerable part of America's high GDP is spent, of course, in ways that do not contribute to a higher standard of living, and in that sense (as in so many other ways) GDP is a misleading measure of well-being. America's expenditures on arms may make the world safer, but arguably, much of this money is wasted. But even if well-spent, it is an investment to maintain the country's standard of living in the future, not part of today's current consumption.

At home, America has been spending huge amounts on prisons. From 1980 to the present day the proportion of state spending on corrections has risen relative to state spending on higher education, with

Massachusetts spending more on prisons than on higher education in 2004.[20] These investments are again included in GDP, but they are symptoms of a dysfunctional society.

Consuming inefficiently (in the broad sense just discussed) is one way to respond to the challenges posed by ever increasing production efficiency. There are clearly better ways.

In the remainder of this essay, I will assume, however, that Americans' real consumption is higher and real leisure is lower than Keynes's analysis would have predicted. I ask, how can we reconcile this American "consumerism" with models of rational behavior?

Conventional and Unconventional Interpretations of the US–EU Comparison

Just as, with some work, one might be able to reconcile the failure of leisure to increase to the extent predicted by Keynes in the United States with the standard model, so too can one attempt to use standard models to explain the lower levels of consumption of leisure in the United States relative to Europe. In US–EU comparison the anomaly is not just that America's seemingly higher wages have not resulted in substantially more leisure but actually in less leisure.

One explanation that critics of the European economic model often raise is that taxes discourage work. But the puzzle is that individuals at similar (*after-tax*) wages seem to work less in Europe, enjoying, for instance, far longer vacations.

Again, with some work, one might be able partially to reconcile these results with conventional theory. For instance, there could be wealth effects, but by most accounts the average American is wealthier than the average European. However, the provision of social services (like health care) may be higher for the average European, and this should have the opposite effect. Countering this argument is the fact that most Americans receive health care benefits from their employer, and these benefits do not depend on the hours worked. The fact that one must work to get these benefits might explain higher labor force participation but not higher hours of those in the labor force.[21]

Some European countries (most notably Sweden) provide assistance to women participating in the labor force, for instance, with generous family leave policies and public support for day care. One would have expected that the provision of these public goods, which are complements to work, would have resulted in *higher* labor force participation

The idea is simple: the value to a husband of a vacation depends on whether his wife can take a vacation at the same time. If not, beyond a brief respite from work, each party would prefer the additional income to staying at home alone, or going on a trip alone. The problem is that the market does not provide a good mechanism for coordinating vacations.

Many European countries have solved the coordination failure problem by having everyone go on vacation at the same time. There are costs associated with this system: capital is idle. But, arguably, the benefits exceed the costs.

There may be some interaction between the magnitude of the coordination failure and the overall demand for leisure. Assume, for instance, that everyone were to take some time off during the month of August. If each person takes one day off, and there is no coordination, then the probability that the two spouses will have the same day off will be very small. (Assume 21 working days, so there is a $1/21$ chance of two persons coordinating their vacation.) If each person takes a full month off, then there is no coordination problem.

There is a parallel argument for the enjoyment of certain other leisure activities. Prior to the television, much of leisure activity was spent in communal activities (e.g., churches). The decrease in time available for these communal activities led to lower participation levels and a decrease in their availability. But this in turn has led to lower enjoyment and a lower demand for communal activities—and a higher demand for goods.[34]

Endogenous Preferences

Failure of Culture as the Solution to the "Resolution" of the Economic Problem   While economists traditionally focus on "economic needs," psychologists emphasize the importance of other basic human needs and pleasures—to solve problems, to feel needed, to experience the pleasure that one gets from seeing a beautiful painting or hearing a musical composition; while our physical needs may be limited (a point especially poignant today, with increasing problems of obesity), our mental and emotional needs are insatiable. It is not even clear that they are subject to the usual laws of diminishing returns. The demand for culture, broadly defined, may be unlimited. In the past, for instance, only a small fraction of our society could enjoy the arts, and, correspondingly, only a small fraction of our population was engaged in the production of the arts. The solution of the "economic" problem means that these pleasures can and should be available more broadly. It was, perhaps, Keynes's hope that this would occur, but it has not, or at least not to the extent that he might have hoped.[35]

The reason can be stated a couple of different ways. We can think of preferences as being endogenous—shaped by a variety of forces that can be studied systematically; or we can think of individuals as learning how to "consume." The two perspectives come to much the same conclusion, though the latter formulation is closer to the standard theory of consumer behavior.

Economists typically assume a fixed set of preferences, but advertising and marketing help shape preferences—and firms have been as inventive in creating new demands as they have been in creating new products. Even food has taken on new dimensions, as consumers seek out exotic foods.[36]

The forces that shape demand in different countries can differ, and thus societies can evolve in different directions. Preferences are, at least in part, socially determined: we are influenced by those around us. In Europe, for instance, there is a growing *slow food movement*, which says that the point of eating is not efficiency, providing the largest number of calories per dollar or in the shortest span of time. The movement sees eating as a pleasure in itself; it is an intellectual activity, combining sensory perceptions with an analysis of the nature of the pleasures to which the senses give rise. It sees cooking as a creative activity and not just a question of how "outsourcing" food preparation to a frozen food company can reduce the time and resources required to transform raw food into food on the table. This movement has far fewer adherents in America.

In the discussion below, I will put forward, in somewhat stark form, the hypothesis that one society can evolve, with endogenous preferences, toward "consumerism," and the other toward a higher preference for leisure.

In each of these two sets of preferences—the one with high preferences for goods, which we refer to as the American model, or the model of consumerism, and the high preference for leisure, which we refer to as the European model—there will be differences in the consequences of improvements in productivity. Going forward, in the American model, one can foresee smaller changes in the levels of work (even possibly increases), but ever increasing levels of consumption. Television screens can become larger and can be put in every room and in both the front and the back of automobiles, and square footage of housing can become ever larger.

As we have noted, the American model works particularly well in a world in which people are especially attuned to differences in income (the kinds of models discussed under hypothesis 1). In such a society the return to targeted advertising can be especially high. If one induces "consumer leaders" to buy SUVs, other consumers will follow.

Learning   In this and the next subsection, I attempt to model endogenous preferences, to formalize the notion that societies can evolve in quite different directions. As I suggested earlier, there are several ways of approaching the problem. In this section, I explore the *learning* hypothesis.

Individuals learn about consuming by consuming (like learning by doing[37]). We learn how to consume from others (at school, from our parents, from our peers), and we are "taught" to consume by others, especially by firms. We can, as a result of this learning, improve the efficiency of consumption, and this can increase the marginal return to consuming.[38]

The enjoyment of cultural and other pleasures of the mind, in particular, does not come easily. A person must be trained. It is work, though not of the physical sort—the toil that used to be required to bring food to the table and to provide basic shelter. Our society has failed to provide the requisite education, which is why so many people get their enjoyment from the modern version of Roman circuses, our television programs and sports.

Markets (monopolistic firms) have an incentive to expand demand (e.g., through advertising) in products in which they have market power. It is, accordingly, not surprising that the multi-million dollar budgets for advertising of movies often equals or exceeds that for the production of the movie itself. For a variety of reasons—not least of which is that much of culture, our heritage of music and art, is in the public domain—there is less market power in "culture," and thus less incentive for *private* firms to provide the "learning."

Learning by Consuming   Even without firms attempting to distort consumption patterns, individuals can learn—they learn how to consume by consuming, they learn how to enjoy leisure by enjoying leisure. This means that *history matters*. Figure 3.1 shows the budget constraint and indifference curve in period 1. But because the individual has

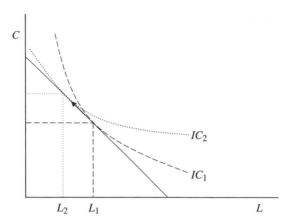

Figure 3.1
Learning by consuming

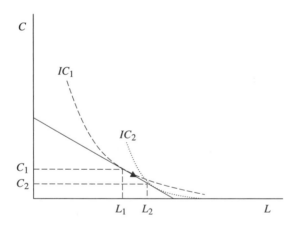

Figure 3.2
Learning by consuming

consumed a lot in this period, and enjoyed little leisure, he is even better at consuming goods in the next period—and less good at enjoying leisure. His indifference curves have tilted so that if his budget constraint were to have remained unchanged, he would have changed his choices, to consume more goods and enjoy less leisure. Over time, even with no changes in wages, consumption increases and leisure decreases.

By contrast, the individual depicted in figure 3.2 has initially the same preferences, but with a lower initial wage, he consumes less.

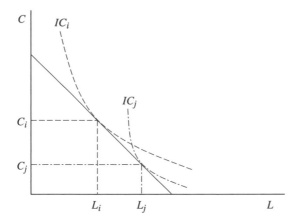

Figure 3.3
Learning by consuming

However, this means that he learns to enjoy leisure more and goods less. Over time, the initial differences in consumption/leisure choices are reinforced.

If, after many periods, the second individual is now confronted with the same wage as the first, his preferences have so changed that markedly different choices are made. Because the second individual is better at enjoying leisure than the first, he enjoys more leisure. (See figure 3.3).[39]

There may be more than one steady state. Figure 3.4 shows a case where, if consumption lies along the rays OA, OB, or OC, marginal rates of transformation remain unchanged with experience. But over time, if individuals consume anywhere between OA and OB, they increasingly come to prefer (at the margin) goods, while between OB and OC, they increasingly come to prefer (at the margin) leisure. This means that once the economy deviates toward more consumption than OB, it increasingly does, eventually converging to some point along the ray OA.

Appendix D formalizes a set of possible dynamics, where consuming more leads to increases in the efficiency of consumption, while enjoying leisure leads to increases in the marginal return to leisure. Whether an increase in the "productivity" of consumption goods leads to an increase or decrease in the marginal utility of consumption depends on whether the elasticity of marginal utility (η) is greater or less than unity. If the elasticities of the marginal utility of goods and leisure

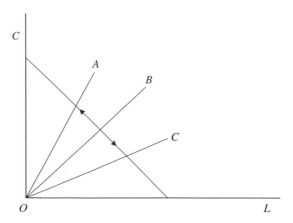

Figure 3.4
Multiple steady states

are both large and if individuals then consume a lot, they demand more consumer goods, and if they enjoy more leisure, the demand for leisure increases: there is a strong centrifugal force.

The dynamics described in the appendix exhibit some interesting properties. The steady state level of labor depends on the rate of increase in wages: it is the adaptation of preferences that drive everything. Again, the steady state may not be stable; it is possible that if the economy deviates from the steady state, it either converges to an equilibrium of extreme consumption or extreme leisure.

Addiction and Myopia   An extreme case of preference formation (or deformation) is illustrated by addiction: having tasted an addictive drug, the individual's trade-offs between that drug and other commodities is changed; often individuals do not know, at the time they first take the addictive drug, what its effects on future preferences will be.

There is now ample evidence that the cigarette companies took advantage of addictive behavior (and even of consumers' lack of knowledge of the addictive characteristics of the products they were being sold). They designed cigarettes to make them *more* addictive, thus increasing their profits—at the expense of individuals' life expectancies, and imposing high medical costs both on those who consumed their products and on the rest of society. The fact that as individuals have become more aware of the addictive properties and health consequences they have changed consumption patterns suggests that indi-

$$\max_{\{L,s\}} U\left(\frac{w(1-s)L}{c_{2,t}}, \frac{wLs(1+r)}{c_{2,t+1}}, L\right).$$

This implies

$$\frac{U_2(1+r)w}{c_{2,t+1}} = \frac{U_1 w}{c_{2,t}},$$

$$\frac{U_1 w(1-s)}{c_{2,t}} + \frac{U_2 ws(1+r)}{c_{2,t+1}} + U_3 = 0,$$

or

$$\frac{U_2(1,1,L^*)}{(1-s^*)} = \frac{U_1(1,1,L^*)}{s^*},$$

$$U_1(1,1,L^*) + U_2(1,1,L^*) + U_3(1,1,L^*)L^* = 0.$$

Neither labor supply nor savings depends on the wage rate.

As a slight generalization of this model, welfare can be represented as a weighted average of a traditional utility function (not dependent on relative consumption) and the relative consumption utility function. Then concern about relative consumption will lead an individual with high leisure–low consumption to work more, and it will lead an individual with low leisure-high consumption to work less.

Appendix C: Implications of Coordination Failures in Leisure

Model C.1

The value of leisure of individual 1 depends on how much leisure individual 2 (spouse) consumes:

$$U = U(C_i, L_i, L_j).$$

If each individual chooses his own leisure (work) independent of others, then

$$\max U(w_i L_i, L_i, L_j).$$

So

$$U_1 w = -U_2, \tag{C.1}$$

or, in the symmetric equilibrium

$$U_1(wL, L, L)w = -U_2(wL, L, L).$$ (C.2)

For simplicity, assume that there are only two groups, 1 and 2. Then (C.1) defines L_1 as a function of L_2 and a symmetric equation defines L_2 as a function of L_1:

$$\frac{dL_1}{dL_2} = -\frac{U_{13}w + U_{23}}{U_{11}w^2 + U_{12}w + U_{21}w + U_{22}}.$$

It is clear that if consumption and leisure are substitutes, but the leisure of the two individuals are complements: the amount worked by individual 1 is an increasing function of that of individual 2, and conversely. Figure 3.5 shows the case where there are multiple equilibria.

In general, there will be underconsumption of leisure. A socially coordinated equilibrium is defined by the solution to

$$U_1 w = -(U_2 + U_3),$$

meaning that even the Nash equilibrium with the most leisure can be improved upon by an increase in leisure. Each individual fails to take into account the effect of the increase of his leisure on the well-being of others.

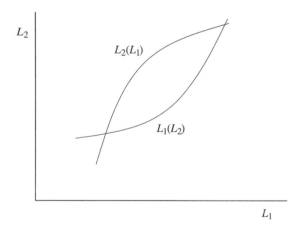

Figure 3.5
Multiple equilibria in leisure

Model C.1a

If we assume that leisures of individual 1 and 2 are perfect complements, and separabililty between consumption and leisure, we have

$U = u(c) - v[\max(L_1, L_2)]$.

Any $L^* \geq L^{**}$, where

$u'(wL^{**})w = v'(L^{**})$,

is an equilibrium, since

$u'w > 0$ for $L < L^*$,

$u'w - v' < 0$ for $L > L^*$.

The equilibrium with the minimum work (maximum leisure) Pareto-dominates, meaning Pareto optimality requires that $L = L^{**}$.

Model C.2

The value of leisure of individual 1 depends on coordinated leisure.

In the previous model it was simply the number of hours worked that mattered, not when individuals took their leisure time. But timing is critical. Assume, for instance, that there are two time periods (vacations in June and July); well-being depends on the coordination of vacations:

$U = U(c, L_1^1, L_1^2, L_2^1, L_2^2)$.

Assume that there are two social arrangements. In one, everyone takes their vacation in the same month and works full time in the other months—the coordinated equilibrium. In the other, the timing of vacations is random.

Assume symmetry. Now it makes no difference whether individuals coordinate on the first or second period. For concreteness, we assume that the utility function takes on the form of

$u(c) + Ev^1[\min L^* - L_1, L^* - L_2] + Ev^2[\min L^* - L_1, L^* - L_2]$,

where each individual assumes that the event that his spouse will have a vacation in the same month will occur with probability 0.5.

The coordinated equilibrium is the solution to

$$wU_c = v',$$

whereas in the uncoordinated equilibrium, half the time there is no (marginal) value to vacation time. So

$$wU_c = 0.5v'$$

It is clear that given the lower (expected) marginal utility of leisure, there will be shorter vacations. Notice that welfare is higher in the coordinated equilibrium.

Appendix D: Learning by Consuming

Assume that individuals learn how to consume by consuming, and how to enjoy leisure by enjoying leisure $(L^* - L)$, but act myopically:

$$U = u(ac) + v[b(L^* - L)].$$

So

$$au'w = v'b. \tag{D.1}$$

Then

$$\alpha + h - \eta[\alpha + h + g] = \beta - \varkappa[\beta - gm], \tag{D.2}$$

where

$$\alpha \equiv \frac{d \ln a}{dt} = \alpha(c), \qquad \alpha' > 0, \alpha = 0, \text{ for } c \geq c^{**}, \tag{D.3}$$

$$\beta \equiv \frac{d \ln b}{dt} = \beta(L^* - L), \qquad \beta' > 0, \tag{D.4}$$

$$\eta \equiv -\frac{d \ln u'}{d \ln c} > 0, \tag{D.5}$$

$$\varkappa \equiv -\frac{d \ln v'}{d \ln[L^* - L]} > 0, \tag{D.6}$$

$$m = \frac{L}{L^* - L} > 0, \tag{D.7}$$

$$g = \frac{d \ln L}{dt}, \tag{D.8}$$

$$h = \frac{d \ln w}{dt}. \tag{D.9}$$

As a result

$$g = \frac{(\alpha + h)(1 - \eta) - \beta(1 - \varkappa)}{\varkappa m + \eta} = 0 \tag{D.10}$$

whenever

$$\beta(L^* - L_e)(1 - \varkappa) = (\alpha(wL_e) + h)(1 - \eta) \tag{D.11}$$

or

$$h = \left[\frac{\beta(1 - \varkappa)}{1 - \eta}\right] - \alpha. \tag{D.12}$$

Likewise

$$\frac{dL_e}{dh} = -\frac{1 - \eta}{\beta'(1 - \varkappa) + \alpha' w(1 - \eta)} \tag{D.13}$$

and

$$\frac{dg}{dL}\bigg|_{g=0} = \frac{\alpha' w(1 - \eta) + \beta'(1 - \varkappa)}{\varkappa m + \eta} > \quad \text{or} \quad < 0 \tag{D.14}$$

as

$$Z = \alpha' w(1 - \eta) + \beta'(1 - \varkappa) > \quad \text{or} \quad < 0.$$

Define $\varsigma = d \ln \alpha / d \ln c$, and $\lambda = d \ln \beta' / d \ln(L - L_e)$. Then

$$Z > \quad \text{or} \quad < 0 \quad \text{as} \quad \varsigma(1 - \eta) + \frac{\lambda(1 - \varkappa)}{m} > \quad \text{or} \quad < 0.$$

It should be clear that standard economic theory puts no restrictions on the sign of Z. For instance, if the utility function is logarithmic in both leisure and consumption, then $Z = 0$ (the borderline case). If $\alpha' = 0$, then sign $= \text{sign}(1 - \varkappa)$.

Thus we have three immediate implications.

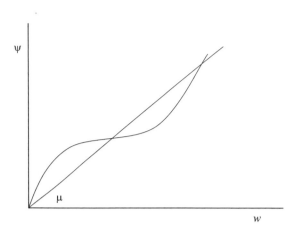

Figure 3.6
Multiple weight equilibria

For simplicity, we focus now on steady states, where

$$\mu w = c. \tag{E.7}$$

Then, substituting, we have

$$\max\ u(t(w)\mu w) - \mu w - V(w).$$

The utility-maximizing level of weight is given by

$$u't\mu[\xi + \mu] - \mu - V' = 0. \tag{E.8}$$

If the marginal cost of obesity is large enough, then myopic consumption leads to excess consumption.

An Example

Assume $u' = (ct)^{-0.5}$. Then

$$u't = t^{0.5}c^{-0.5} = 1 \tag{E.9}$$

implies that

$$c = t(w). \tag{E.10}$$

Let

$$t = w^2. \tag{E.11}$$

Then the steady state weight is

$$w^* = \mu. \tag{E.12}$$

On the other hand, the optimal steady state weight is the solution to

$$(\mu + 2)(ct)^{-0.5}t\mu = \mu + V',$$

or

$$(\mu + 2)\psi^{0.5}w^{0.5} = \mu + V'.$$

Consider the value at w^* of the derivative of steady state utility with respect to w:

$$(\mu + 2)w - [\mu + V'].$$

So a sufficient condition for the optimal weight being less than w^* is simply that

$$V'(\mu) > \mu^2 + \mu.$$

Appendix F: Limitations of Standard Analyses

The question why Europeans on average enjoy more leisure than Americans has attracted the attention of several scholars.[42] Using standard neoclassical models, they have attempted, for instance, to ascertain whether differences can be explained by differences in tax rates or unionization and regulation. Most of the "standard analyses" use special parameterizations and ignore essential features of labor markets. While they may provide "rigorous" proofs of labor market responses to, say, increases in taxes or unionization, the analyses are of only limited relevance to understanding actual labor market behavior. This appendix calls attention to some of the critical limitations of these analyses. In many cases, introducing these elements of realism introduces ambiguity into even the qualitative predictions.

Uncertainty

The standard model pays no attention to uncertainty and differences in risk in different countries, such as differences in the strength of the social safety net. Long-standing theories of household behavior under uncertainty are used to explain why the response to uncertainty may be large but may be of uncertain sign. On the one hand, individuals may work more (if they are very consumption risk averse). Moreover there may be an increase in labor force participation if households want to be sure that at least one member of the household always is employed. On the other hand, wage uncertainty may reduce the attractiveness of participating in the labor force (e.g., in choosing between working in the market or nonmarket sector, since an increase in the risk of market labor reduces the attractiveness of market labor relative to nonmarket labor).

America's weaker social safety net may explain some of the greater labor force participation (a greater need for precautionary saving and a greater need to be sure that at least one member of the household is engaged in the labor market[43]).

Unionization

Some analyses within the standard model argue that stronger unions in Europe have driven up wages and thereby lowered employment. Because of their monopoly power they have, in effect, created the problem of unemployment and low labor force participation. There are several crucial errors in the standard analysis.[44]

Local Bargaining

First, the standard analysis assumes that in the absence of unions, there would be perfectly competitive labor markets, with perfect information and complete risk markets, and the other attributes of the perfect markets paradigm so that, in particular, in the absence of unions, labor markets would clear. One of the major developments in the analysis of labor markets in the last several decades is an understanding that many workers face small-scale bargaining problems with their employers. The labor market is thus better described as characterized by bilateral monopoly and/or monopoly/monopsonistic competition than by models of perfect competition. There may be large search costs associated with finding another job, uncertainty about the myriad of important nonpecuniary characteristics, and uncertainty about the myriad of relevant skills possessed by the employee. Hiring and training costs can be significant. Insider/outsider theory has explained why insiders may be reluctant to train outsiders. Most of the relevant risks are uninsurable, and not surprising, given all of these limitations, the market equilibrium is not in general Pareto efficient.[45]

Moreover, once hired, the worker's pay is only partially related to his labor supply (effort). Typically a worker's pay depends on a host of other factors, including the performance of others.[46] This means, in particular, that returns to labor supply are risky, with the ambiguous effects noted earlier.

Unions may play an important role in *correcting* (or at least offsetting) these market failures, for instance, in attempting to get contractual arrangements with better risk sharing between employees and employers. As a result it is not obvious that, *in theory*, unionization would necessarily lead to less work.

Flawed Theory of Monopoly Power

Much of the standard analysis is, in particular, based on the old fashioned theory of monopoly, where in order to receive a higher price, supply is restricted. But more than three decades ago, it became clear that there were serious flaws in this theory.[47] In particular, a perfectly discriminating monopolist would not introduce any distortions in resource allocation; the only distortions arise from limitations in the ability to discriminate—limitations, for instance, that arise from imperfections of information. Unions, in particular, are able to (and in fact do) sign complicated, non-linear contracts with firms.[48] These contracts may or may not result in reduced labor supply[49] (by reducing risk, they may indeed, as noted earlier, increase workers' labor supply); in any case, the argument that they reduce labor supply should be based on a more sophisticated analysis of monopoly power.[50]

For instance, while unions may have worked to ensure that workers face less risk (so that firms bear more of the risk than they otherwise would have), it is not obvious that when they succeed in doing so (with appropriately designed contracts), labor supply is less than it would otherwise have been.[51]

By the same token, most observers believe that unions have been a force for equalitarianism, compressing the wage structure from what it otherwise would have been. The effect of wage compression on aggregate labor supply, in turn, depends on the concavity or convexity of labor supply functions.

In short, even if unions succeed in obtaining more rents for their workers, the distortions in the labor supply may be limited. If, however, unions do succeed in getting for their workers a larger share

As I note in the text, some forms of public expenditure (like retirement benefits) are closely linked with contributions; presumably the
shift from the private to the public sector has little effect on labor supply. To the extent that individuals are "forced" to save more than they
otherwise would like, there may be some effect on labor supply, but
the effect is of ambiguous sign. To the extent that public programs are
more efficient than private programs, the effect of the shift is to increase real wages, with the effect on labor supply depending on the
elasticity of labor supply with respect to wages.

Similarly, to the extent that expenditures on public investment goods
increase labor productivity (i.e., $w = w(g)$, where g is the level of public
expenditure), then the effect of increased public expenditures depends
again on the labor supply elasticity.[58] To the extent that the utility
of public goods expenditures are separable from leisure, then these
expenditures may have little effect on labor supply, and the standard
analyses (ignoring expenditure effects) apply directly.

Finally, to the extent that public revenue is spent to redistribute
income,[59] the effects are complex. Individual payments (benefits) that
depend on before-tax incomes give rise to complicated patterns
of effective marginal tax rates, for instance, with negative marginal
tax rates on very low-income individuals (with the earned income tax
credit) and very high marginal tax rates on low-income individuals. At
the same time, income effects lead to less labor supply (than otherwise
would have been the case) among low-income individuals (the benefi-
ciaries of the redistributions) and higher labor supplies among high-
income individuals partially offset each other.

Progressive Taxation

Generally, progressive taxation, with marginal tax rates exceeding average tax rates, imply that the adverse effect of taxes is greater than it
otherwise would be because the substitution effect is larger. One way
of thinking about the consequences is to consider a simple linear income tax with a surtax. Then those in the surtax range have a linear
budget constraint,

$$C = a + bw(1 - t)L,$$

with an intercept (a) for higher income individuals that is higher than
that for lower income individuals, so that the implied income effect on
upper income individuals partially leads to lower levels of labor
supply.

Aggregation

Precise aggregation (consistent with using a representative agent model, e.g., with labor supply depending only on average wages) requires labor supply functions that are linear in wages and income. This is only true for highly restrictive conditions. For instance, in the log log formulation of employment, individuals maximize

$$\ln(wL + I) + a \ln(L^* - L).$$

So

$$\frac{w}{wL + I} = \frac{a}{L^* - L},$$

or

$$wL^* - wL = awL + aI,$$

or

$$L = \frac{wL^* - aI}{(1 + a)w}.$$

While labor supply is linear in I, it is not linear in w. (It is linear in $1/w$). Indeed

$$EL = \frac{L^*}{1 + a} - \frac{aI}{1 + a} E \frac{1}{w}$$

Because labor supply is a concave function of w, the greater the wage dispersion, the lower is the labor supply. Differences in wage dispersions across countries or changes over time can affect aggregate labor supply.

Notes

I am deeply indebted to Stephan Litschig, Gustavo Piga, and Lorenzo Pecchi for helpful comments.

1. In current income, world GDP in 2006 was $48 trillion; in purchasing power parity, some $67 trillion. See *World Development Indicators 2007*, World Bank: Washington, DC.

2. The poverty line for a family of four in America in 2008 was $21,200. *Federal Register* 73(15), January 23, 2008, pp. 3971–72.

3. *Global Economic Prospects 2007*, World Bank: Washington, DC, p. xiii.

4. This is, of course, beyond the changes that one would have expected from moving from a manufacturing economy to a service-sector "knowledge" economy (akin to the structural changes that confronted the economy as it moved from agriculture to industry).

5. The average number of hours spent watching television per year for individuals aged 18 and over in the United States in 2003 is estimated at 1,745 hours and projected to rise to 1,931 hours by 2008. That is equivalent to approximately 35 (38) hours per week— roughly as much as individuals spend in the labor force. US Census Bureau, *Statistical Abstract of the United States*, 2006, tab. 1116.

6. See G. Faggio and S. Nickell, 2006, Patterns of work across the OECD, CEP discussion paper 730, tabs. 3 and 4. This is consistent with Aguiar and Hurst who find "market" work to have increased slightly from 28 hours a week to 29 hours in the United States. See M. Aguiar and E. Hurst, 2006, Measuring trends in leisure: The allocation of time over 5 decades, Federal Reserve Bank of Boston working paper 06-2. It seems to make the most sense to look at average hours worked per person of working age, as opposed to average hours worked per person employed (which has decreased in both the United States and Europe). One reason is that the decision to enjoy more leisure may be reflected in more leisure during working years or fewer working years (entering the labor force at a later date, leaving it at an earlier date), and the latter would not be captured by hours worked by people in employment. Similarly, while the employed may work less, more people of working age may actually be working.

From 1970 to 2000, hours worked per person did not decrease, but increased by 26 percent. The difference between the two statistics is related to changes in demography. O. Blanchard, 2004, The economic future of Europe. NBER working paper 10310.

7. G. Faggio and S. Nickell, 2006, Patterns of work across the OECD, CEP discussion paper 730.

8. A. F. Alesina, E. L. Glaeser, and B. Sacerdote, 2005, Work and leisure in the US and Europe: Why so different? CEPR discussion paper 5140.

9. J. K. Galbraith, 1958, *The Affluent Society*, London, Hamish Hamilton.

10. Aguiar and Hurst, note 6.

11. For instance, there may be differences in norms concerning workplace socialization. Moreover patterns of socialization outside the workplace may affect the value of socialization in the workplace. For a discussion of the marked changes in patterns of communal activities in the United States, see R. Putnam, 2000, *Bowling Alone: The Collapse and Revival of American Community*, New York, Simon and Schuster. The absence of comparable studies for Europe makes it difficult to assess the importance of such explanations.

12. J. E. Morton and I. V. Sawhill, 2007, *Economic Mobility: Is the American Dream Alive and Well?* Washington, DC, Economic Mobility Project, Pew Charitable Trusts.

13. It depends on the concavity (convexity) of the demand for leisure as a function of wages and "full" income (wealth). Alesina et al., note 8, present data showing that an increase in the Gini coefficient is associated with an increase in average hours worked. See also appendix F.

14. Faggio and Nickell, note 7, tab. 3.

15. Among OECD countries in 2004, the United States is only average in terms of female labor force participation, Faggio and Nickell, note 7, tab. 3.

16. Putnam, note 11, documents these marked changes in patterns of life. A household survey of adolescents in Minneapolis showed that in the course of a week, one out of seven never ate with their families, and one out of three ate with their families twice or less a week. D. Neumark-Sztainer, P. J. Nahhan, M. Story, J. Croll, and C. Perry, 2003, Family meal patterns: Associations with sociodemographic characteristics and improved dietary intake among adolescents, *Journal of the American Dietetic Association* 103: 317–22.

17. See Alesina et al., note 8; P. R. G. Layard, 2005, *Happiness, Lessons from a New Science*, New York, Penguin Press; R. Frank, 1999, *Luxury Fever: Money and Happiness in an Era of Excess*, New York, Free Press.

18. See Putnam, note 11.

19. To be sure, however, there are other factors that have contributed.

20. Massachusetts spent $1,030 million on corrections in 2005 and $987 million on higher education. National Association of State Budget Officers, 2006, *State Expenditure Report, Fiscal Year 2005*.

21. Also, since what matters is the availability of family group health insurance, all that is required is that one member of the household be in the labor force. Hence America's health care system can explain greater labor force participation only to the extent that the primary earner does not have health insurance with his employer and/or to the extent that there are more households with only one potential earner. In both Europe and the United States, the elderly receive health benefits whether they work or not.

Higher social security benefits, by the same token, provide an explanation only to the extent that the benefits are unrelated to contributions. Both in the United States and Europe there is a close linkage between the two, and the strength of the linkage has increased more in Europe in recent years than in the United States; this, according to the standard theory, should have resulted in a relative increase in European labor supply.

The close linkage between benefits and contributions means, of course, that it is inappropriate to view the social security contribution as a tax. So long as the requisite savings are less than what individuals would have done on their own account, there is no effect on labor supply. When the implied compulsory savings exceeds that which individuals would have done on their own account, the effects on labor supply are ambiguous, because of the implied conflicting substitution and income effects (the forced saving reduces the marginal return to work). See J. E. Stiglitz, Taxation, public policy and the dynamics of unemployment, *International Tax and Public Finance* 6: 239–62 (paper presented to the Institute of International Finance, Cordoba, Argentina, August 24, 1998).

There are other effects not taken into account in most of the standard models trying to explain patterns of leisure (e.g., Alesina et al., note 8): for instance, differences in risk and in the strength of safety nets will have potentially significant effects both on labor force participation when labor supply is a household decision (see K. Basu, G. Genicot, and J. E. Stiglitz, 2002, Minimum wage laws and unemployment benefits, in K. Basu, P. Nayak, and R. B. Ray, eds., *Markets and Governments*, New York, Oxford University Press, ch. 3) and on hours worked (see M. Rothschild and J. E. Stiglitz, 1971, Increasing risk: II. Its economic consequences, *Journal of Economic Theory* 5(1): 66–84). Theoretically the effects are complicated and ambiguous. The absence of safety nets has been thought to lead Americans to work more in order to have a larger precautionary savings buffer, but in fact most lower income Americans have little savings (other than the net worth of their house).

22. See Alesina et al., note 8, for an overview of this literature. While there are larger labor supply elasticities for secondary earners, typically this reflects marked shifts from home production to market production with the entry of women into the labor force.

23. S. Nickell, 2004, Employment and taxes, CEP discussion paper 634.

24. This is the general result of several studies that have looked at this issue. See, for example, Faggio and Nickell, note 7. The studies do not make clear whether they have netted out that part of social security contributions that are directly linked with benefits. This would presumably lower tax rates in Europe, markedly increasing the magnitude of the puzzle.

25. E. C. Prescott, 2004, Why do Americans work so much more than Europeans? *Federal Reserve Bank of Minneapolis Quarterly Review* 28(1): 2–13.

26. See Aguiar and Hurst, note 6.

27. As always, matters are more complicated. Since wages at the bottom have declined and those elsewhere have increased, these patterns suggest a positive supply elasticity at the bottom, and a negative supply elasticity at the top. This is, of course, consistent with the standard backward bending labor supply curve.

28. Empirical studies trying to take into account effective marginal tax rates face several complexities. As noted elsewhere, old age contributions are related to benefits, and it is only the difference that should be viewed as a tax. In the United States married low-wage earners with children receive a large earned income tax credit, which means they face a large *negative* tax rate, while those with slightly higher incomes face a very large positive marginal tax rate, higher than even high-income Americans.

29. See E. F. P. Luttmer, 2005, Neighbors as negatives: Relative earnings and well-being, *Quarterly Journal of Economics* 120(3): 963–1002.

30. While such a conclusion may seem obvious to most, much of modern standard economic theory has argued to the contrary: it has explored models (e.g., representative agent models with fixed preferences and technology) in which there is a unique long-run equilibrium, to which the economy converges, regardless of initial conditions (history).

31. For simplicity, I refer to the "high-consumption" patterns of behavior as the "American model."

32. This particular hypothesis would presumably suggest that lower income Americans should work particularly more than their European counterparts, but the anomalous patterns are particularly marked among higher income Americans. But it may be that those at the bottom have dropped out of the race; the effects of the race appear only among the more educated Americans. (For an explanation why those at the bottom may drop out of the race, see B. Nalebuff and J. E. Stiglitz, 1983, Prizes and incentives: Toward a general theory of compensation and competition, *Bell Journal* 14(1): 21–43.

33. The parallel between this "excess consumption" and signaling/screening equilibrium (where individuals may spend more on education or work harder than they otherwise would) should be clear. See, in particular, J. E. Stiglitz, 2002, Information and the change in the paradigm in economics (abbreviated version of Nobel lecture), *American Economic Review* 92(3): 460–501, and G. Akerlof, 1976, The economics of caste and of the rat race and other woeful tales, *Quarterly Journal of Economics* 90(4): 599–617.

Some economists have suggested that Europeans intrinsically may have been just as focused on consumption (on *relative* consumption) as Americans, but having fallen behind, they have now abandoned the contest. This explanation, however, is unpersuasive: to the extent that individuals do pay attention to relative consumption, it is the consumption of those that they encounter on a regular basis. I think that there are alternative and more persuasive explanations, based on the recognition that the cost of winning this game—both to the individuals involved and to society more generally—is too high. This again raises the question of why Europeans would be more cognizant of these costs—and given that the disparity in the consumption of leisure is of more recent vintage, why differences in perceptions should have developed in recent decades. The theory presented as hypothesis 3 forms a part of the explanation.

34. See Putnam, note 11.

35. Earlier I noted that a substantial fraction of incremental consumption has been for education, travel, and other complements to leisure. This is, of course, not inconsistent with the view that markets have encouraged activities with which there are associated profits; those forms of leisure, such as classical music, where profit opportunities are more limited, have not increased commensurately.

Some economists have suggested that the demand for certain types of "culture" may be a signaling device by which the rich and well-educated can enable their children to be identified, since those who do not get trained to appreciate, say, classical music, in their youth face far higher costs in learning to enjoy such music later in life. In that sense, part of the demand for culture may be a reflection of utility dependent on relative status.

36. Some think of advertising as providing information which alters choices; others as trying to change preferences directly.

37. K. J. Arrow, 1962, The economic implications of learning by doing, *Review of Economic Studies* 29(3): 155–73.

38. As always, matters are more complex. If our utility of goods is represented by $U(aC)$, where a is a measure of the "efficiency" of consumption, then the marginal utility of consumption is $aU'(ac)$, and an increase in a (which always increases the *utility* of consumption) decreases or increases the *marginal* utility of consumption as $-d \ln U'/d \ln C >$ or < 1 (since if U is concave then $U'' < 0$ and $d \ln U'/d \ln C < 0$).

39. Atkinson and Stiglitz formulated the concept of localized technological progress: firms learn how to produce better *at the technologies at which they are producing*, but knowledge about other technologies may be relatively unchanged. So here too we can think of localized preference deformation: individuals may change their marginal rate of substitution of leisure for goods at their current (and neighboring) levels of well-being (indifference curves), but preferences at other levels of well-being may be relatively unchanged. By contrast, in the models explored here, preference changes are global in nature. See A. B. Atkinson and J. E. Stiglitz, 1969, A new view of technological change, *Economic Journal* 79(315): 573–78.

40. Some economists have tried to use data from "happiness" surveys to ascertain whether those who work less (taking into account the reduced income that lower work results in) are happier. Alesina et al. (note 8) conclude, for instance, that "this evidence at least suggests that Europeans seem to be happy to work less and less." See also Layard, note 17, and Frank, note 17. These studies also confirm the direct positive impact on happiness of employment and the negative impact of job insecurity.

41. Much of the testing of "rationality" is exploring a much weaker hypothesis: Are individuals sensitive (in the predicted way) to changes in prices? As I have argued elsewhere, individuals could exhibit price sensitivity without being fully rational. See, for example,

J. E. Stiglitz, 1989, Rational peasants, efficient institutions and the theory of rural organization: Methodological remarks for development economics, in P. Bardhan, ed., *The Economic Theory of Agrarian Institutions*, Oxford, Clarendon Press, pp. 18–29.

42. See, for instance, Alesina et al., note 8, or Prescott, note 25.

43. However, the lower unemployment rate in the United States will mitigate against the need for "precautionary" labor force participation.

44. The differences in hours per worker between Europe and the United States are greater than can be explained by differences in unemployment rates.

45. See, for instance, R. Arnott and J. E. Stiglitz, 1985, Labor turnover, wage structure and moral hazard: The inefficiency of competitive markets, *Journal of Labor Economics* 3(4): 434–62; B. Greenwald and J. E. Stiglitz, 1988, Pareto inefficiency of market economies: Search and efficiency wage models, *American Economic Review* 78(2): 351–55.

46. See J. E. Stiglitz, 1975, Incentives, risk and information: Notes toward a theory of hierarchy, *Bell Journal of Economics* 6(2): 552–79.

47. See J. E. Stiglitz, 1977, Monopoly, non-linear pricing and imperfect information: The insurance market, *Review of Economic Studies* 44(3): 407–30.

48. See, for instance, J. E. Stiglitz, 1987, Design of labor contracts: Economics of incentives and risk-sharing, in H. Nalbantian, ed., *Incentives, Cooperation and Risk Sharing*, Totowa, NJ, Rowman and Allanheld, pp. 47–68.

49. The argument is analogous to that put forward by Cheung, on why sharecropping may not affect labor supply, even though the fact that the landlord gets 50 percent (or in some cases, two-thirds) of the *marginal* output would, in the standard models, have suggested a large reduction in labor supply. See S. Cheung, 1968, Private property rights and share-cropping, *Journal of Political Economy* 76(6): 1107–22; and S. Cheung, 1969, *The Theory of Share Tenancy*, Chicago, University of Chicago Press.

50. By the same token, David Card and Alan Krueger have argued that minimum wages have not led to a reduction in the level of employment. See D. Card and A. Krueger, 1994, Minimum wages and employment: A case study of the fast-food industry in New Jersey and Pennsylvania, *American Economic Review* 84(4): 772–93. See also D. Card and A. B. Krueger, 1995, *Myth and Measurement*, Princeton, Princeton University Press.

51. Of course, even if labor supply is reduced, well-being may be increased, such as because of the solution to the coordination problems discussed in relation to hypothesis 3 or because of the reduction in uncertainty. Countervailing the monopoly power of unions (which itself would have led to lower output than otherwise) may also lead to welfare gains.

52. See J. E. Stiglitz, 1987, The causes and consequences of the dependence of quality on prices, *Journal of Economic Literature* 25: 1–48.

53. For an overview of efficiency wage models, and the relationship between these models and standard economic theory, see Stiglitz, The causes and consequences of the dependence of quality on prices, note 52, and J. E. Stiglitz, 1986, Theories of wage rigidities, in J. L. Butkiewicz et al., eds., *Keynes' Economic Legacy: Contemporary Economic Theories*, New York, Praeger, pp. 153–206. Earlier studies of efficiency wage models include J. E. Stiglitz, 1974, Alternative theories of wage determination and unemployment in L.D.C.'s: The labor turnover model, *Quarterly Journal of Economics* 88(2): 194–227; J. E. Stiglitz,

1976, The efficiency wage hypothesis, surplus labor and the distribution of income in L.D.C.'s, *Oxford Economic Papers* 28(2): 185–207; J. E. Stiglitz, 1982, Alternative theories of wage determination and unemployment: The efficiency wage model, in M. Gersovitz et al., eds., *The Theory and Experience of Economic Development: Essays in Honor of Sir Arthur W. Lewis*, London, Allen and Unwin, pp. 78–106; J. E. Stiglitz, 1987, The wage-productivity hypothesis: Its economic consequences and policy implications, In M. J. Boskin, ed., *Modern Developments in Public Finance*, Oxford, Blackwell, pp. 130–65; B. Nalebuff, A. Rodriguez, and J. E. Stiglitz, 1993, Equilibrium unemployment as a worker screening device, NBER working paper 4357; and C. Shapiro and J. E. Stiglitz, 1984, Equilibrium unemployment as a worker discipline device, *American Economic Review* 74(3): 433–44.

54. As noted several times earlier, higher unemployment rates in Europe explain only a fraction of the differences in aggregate labor supply. Europeans also enjoy, for instance, longer vacations and shorter average work weeks. These job attributes may be an efficient way of increasing the net rents associated with employment, thereby reducing the risk of shirking. As I note below, the more myopic behavior of American firms (higher implicit discount rates, greater focus on the current bottom line; see J. E. Stiglitz, 2003, *Roaring Nineties*, New York, Norton) can lead to lower real wages and higher turnover costs.

55. See P. Rey and J. E. Stiglitz, 1993, Moral hazard and unemployment in competitive equilibrium, unpublished manuscript, University of Toulouse (revised July 1996).

56. See, for example, B. Greenwald and J. E. Stiglitz, 2003, Macroeconomic fluctuations in an economy of Phelps-Winter markets, in P. Aghion, R. Frydman, J. Stiglitz, and M. Woodford, eds., *Knowledge, Information, and Expectations in Modern Macroeconomics: In Honor of Edmund S. Phelps*, Princeton, Princeton University Press, pp. 123–36.

57. See, for example, Prescott, note 25.

58. That is, assume that $g = twL = th(g)L(w^*)$, where after-tax wage $w^* = (1-t)h(g)$, so $g = th(g)(L((1-t)h(g))$. Hence $dg/dt = \{hL - th^2L'\}/\{1 - th'[L + hL'(1-t)]$, and $dw^*/dt = -h + (1-t)h' \, dg/dt$. The standard analysis only focuses on the first term and ignores the second term. Analyses that assume that tax revenues are spent on goods that are perfect substitutes for private goods imply that there is an adverse income effect.

59. Representative agent models, of course, simply assume away these effects.

4 Whose Grandchildren?

Robert Solow

Although it was not published until 1930, Keynes's essay was written early in 1928 and read to a student society at Winchester (an elite public school, maybe slightly more intellectual and slightly less aristocratic than Keynes's own Eton). Keynes's biographer, Robert Skidelsky, tells us that the piece was revised and read at other places before it was finally published.

In 1928 the *Economic Journal*, which Keynes edited, published Frank Ramsey's famous article "A Theory of Saving." That was an attempt to analyze how rapidly a community ought to accumulate capital and increase consumption. To make the mathematics work, Ramsey had to assume that the representative household could be effectively satiated with consumer goods. He called this state of affairs Bliss. Keynes uses the same word here. It is a fair guess that this essay was stimulated in part by Ramsey's investigation (which, the story goes, Keynes had suggested to him).

This is not irrelevant information. Keynes was aware of the Great Depression by 1930, but much of the "waste and confusion" he mentions must relate to England's prolonged economic troubles that were already a source of worry in the second half of the 1920s. The Keynes who wrote *Economic Possibilities* had not yet begun to work out the systematic ideas that became the *General Theory*. That book was primarily short-run macroeconomics, but its conceptual framework would have helped him to think about the long-run issues in *Economic Possibilities*, if only through the advantages that come with a systematic accounting for national income, consumption, investment and saving.

It is probably better to treat this essay, especially given its origin, as a *jeu d'esprit*, an occasion to speculate freely, cleverly, and even shockingly to a roomful of bright schoolboys, future bankers, and high civil servants. As Skidelsky says, Keynes preferred that sort of exercise to the more formal, constricted style of writing that was necessary in addressing an audience of economists. Nevertheless, I think we have to read the essay also as the work of an economist. It lays some claim—only some—to professional authority.

With this in mind, I propose to reflect on a handful of questions. What exactly was Keynes predicting about the future, about 2030? Will he turn out to have been right, or nearly so? In any case, was it a sound prediction, given what he could have known at the time he made it? And what did he have to say that is relevant to the economic possibilities for *our* grandchildren? We have to include among his "predictions" his firmly held ideas about the social and moral consequences of early and late capitalism, because those—like the role of entrepreneurial energy, greed, and systematic invidiousness—were certainly a part of the possibilities offered to distant future generations. These more general reflections were the main focus of his essay, but I want to make some connections to the economics in the background.

Keynes's general remarks about the long centuries of slow or nonexistent growth and the role of technical progress and capital accumulation sound very modern (although my private consultant on economic history tells me that he dates the beginnings of "modern" growth too early). The story he tells in a few paragraphs reminds one of Robert Lucas's remark that once you begin to think about economic growth, it is hard to think about anything else. Nevertheless, with three-quarters of the century already gone by, one does not quite feel that "mankind is solving its economic problem." Far from it. What went wrong?

He puts the annual rate of growth of the capital stock at about 2 percent, which might even be a little slow. And he says that "technical efficiency" increases by at least 1 percent per year. (Let us suppose, anachronistically, that he meant total factor productivity here. He was a clever man.) The standard calculation would then have aggregate output growing at, say, 1.7 percent per year. Grant Keynes's assumption, made only for convenience, that population levels off. Then, after a hundred years, output per person will have multiplied 5.4 times. Raise the annual growth rate to 2 percent, and the growth factor after a century is 7.2. The numbers hang together.

Of course, the world's population has not been level since 1930, not nearly, and that accounts for much of the failure to "solve the economic problem." One can say: Oh, well, it was just for the sake of a quick calculation; the adjustment to a growing population is easy to make.

True, but I think the discrepancy also reflects something unattractive in Keynes and his circle. "Mankind" in that sentence quoted above does not seem to include Africans, Asians, Latin Americans, maybe not even southern Europeans. The "our grandchildren" of the title seem tacitly to be limited to the descendants of well-born, educated Englishmen. If this omission had been brought to his attention, Keynes would certainly have acknowledged it and made conventional noises. But the implicit narrowness of scope is there in the background.

The mere arithmetic of population growth is not the whole point. In much of the interval since 1930, the processes of capital accumulation and technical progress skipped over those large parts of the world for reasons that development economists still argue about, and that still operate. Most of that world's grandchildren are pretty poor, and will still be poor in 2030.

There is also a technical growth-theoretic glitch in Keynes's calculation. He starts by projecting into the far future the rough empirical judgment that the stock of real capital accumulates at a rate of 2 percent a year. If capital as a productive input is subject to diminishing returns, however, it may not be possible to keep the capital stock growing that fast, not even if all of output were invested. Under the assumptions about technology normally adopted by economists today, it will not be possible forever, and probably not for a century. To reach Keynes's conclusion, the rate of technical progress would have to be faster than he thinks it is. (It probably is a little faster, now.) This is another reason why he is too optimistic about the grandchildren's prospects, even his friends' grandchildren.

Still, one has to give him credit for understanding, at an unpromising time, that the longer run trajectory of developed capitalist economies depends on the forces of investment and innovation, and also for seeing, though imperfectly, how the story might work itself out.

I will come back to some background issues of economics later, but first I want to turn to those matters that were really on Keynes's mind when he addressed the Essay Society at Winchester. He was arguing that sooner or later, if not in one century then in two, the march of capital accumulation and technical progress will have enabled "us"— whoever "we" are—to produce all the marketable goods and services we need, and with very little effort. How will we spend our time then and, more tellingly, what will motivate us?

In the days before the economic problem had been "solved," activities like working, saving, investing, and inventing were indispensable for economic progress. And they were kept going, in a market economy, by what Keynes called "money-grubbing." There is nothing intrinsically wrong with working or inventing, for instance. Mozart worked and Newton invented. What Keynes found distasteful was greed, the love of money, and they were—and are—the drivers of the processes that drive capitalism.

He is eloquent about his dislike of this way of life, maybe a little over the top. The love of money is "a somewhat disgusting morbidity, one of those semi-criminal, semi-pathological propensities which one hands over with a shudder to the specialists in mental disease." (He is not above some polite anti-semitism on this subject, nor is he above casual error: immortality plays no special role in Jewish thought.) Since these repugnant motives will not be necessary after 2030, what could appear in their place? And what does the experience of the past 75 years of rising incomes tell us about what seems likely to appear in their place?

Keynes's hope is that "we" will occupy our leisure by cultivating what are usually called the finer things in life. There is no need to be too hoity-toity about this. It doesn't have to be all Mozart and Newton and Raphael and Proust, though reverse snobbery is not so attractive either. Perhaps pushpin is not as good as poetry, but playfulness is certainly part of the good life. We don't know if Keynes was broadminded about Everyman's use of leisure, but the rest of us can enjoy the World Cup with good conscience.

It is sort of amusing that Keynes did not, perhaps could not, foresee the burgeoning growth of the entertainment industry: film, television, DVDs, popular music, tourism, golf. The profit motive that he so disdained is filling the leisure time he was worried about.

The real thrust of the essay is not so much the specific uses of all that leisure, as long as they are nondestructive, as it is the motives and the frame of mind that govern choices. Keynes's real worry is that the grandchildren may not be able to shake off the acquisitiveness, the conspicuous consumption, the narrowness of purpose that may perform a useful function at current levels of productivity but will be merely unpleasant in the future. He does not find much comfort in contemplating the behavior of the already rich in 1930. That is why he thinks there is a problem. He claims to be optimistic about the future, but he would not think there had been an improvement up to the present day.

Naturally a lot of this concern sounds hollow in a world in which many millions of people live on less than $2 a day, or even in Europe and North America where mere millions have trouble paying for adequate food, shelter, and health care. Keynes's utter lack of interest in distributional matters is a serious flaw. But that is not adequate reason to ignore the particular challenge that occupied him. Even at today's productivity levels, let alone those another century from now, it is legitimate to wonder why anyone with a billion dollars would want to have two. If the answer is that it is greed for power or preeminence rather than sheer wealth, that only makes the desire more repugnant and more dangerous. The justification that the search for the extra billion contributes to economic efficiency lacks conviction. Even if it did, Keynes's point is that a little extra efficiency might not be worth the accompanying disfigurement of human motives. And, I might add, it doesn't do much for equity either.

This brings me to a last comment, an economist's comment. In speaking of the attraction of having at least some useful work to do, Keynes traces this to "the old Adam," to remembered habit. He would presumably have been glad to allow something for the instinct of workmanship: that may actually be one of the finer things in life. But in the grandchildren's world he imagines, not much useful work will be required: he mentions a fifteen-hour week, and even then as a concession to habit. This is another indication of how far off Keynes's timing was. Counting a four-week vacation for everyone, that would be 720 hours of work per year, less than half of the current average in western Europe, and considerably less than half in the contemporary United States. I already have one grandchild who works a full week, and the younger ones will do much the same. Labor productivity will increase further during the next twenty years, but annual hours of work seem unlikely to fall anywhere near Keynes's estimate.

Where did he go wrong? This is not a simple matter. Economists argue today about the substantial current difference in hours worked between the United States and Europe: Does it reflect cultural differences in attitudes toward consumption and leisure or more pedestrian differences in the financial incentive to work provided by patterns of compensation and taxation? But Keynes must have missed something common to both sides of the Atlantic. Maybe, in common with economists generally, he thought of "leisure" as an alternative to consumption, whereas in reality it is an adjunct to consumption. You can listen

5   Corporatism and Keynes: His Philosophy of Growth

Edmund S. Phelps

Of the main contests in twentieth-century political economy, the contest between capitalism and corporatism still matters. And it matters quite a lot, as I believe the recent economic record of continental western Europe helps to confirm.[1] My discussion here of the economic thought of John Maynard Keynes will focus on his early "corporatist" dissatisfaction with the market—a dissatisfaction that ran deeper than the Pigovian critique of *laissez faire*, later known as the "free market" system.

Intellectual Currents in Keynes's Day

Before we can discuss Keynes in relation to corporatism and capitalism we have to ask: What do they mean now? And in what ways did their meaning differ in Keynes's day?

Today a predominantly capitalist economy, whatever its minor deviations from the ideal type, means a private-ownership system marked by great *openness* to the *new commercial ideas* and the *personal knowledge* of private entrepreneurs and, further, by great *pluralism* in the *private knowledge* and *idiosyncratic views* among the wealth-owners and financiers who select the ideas to which to provide capital and incentives for their development.[2]

A corporatist economy today is a private-ownership system with some contrasting features: It is pervaded with most or all of the economic institutions created or built up by the system called *corporatavismo* that arose in interwar Italy: big employer confederations, big labor unions and monopolistic banks—with a large state bureaucracy to monitor, intervene, and mediate among them. Yet without some knowledge of the purposes for which the system was constructed it cannot be understood at all adequately.

I think it is fair to say that the core function of the distinctive corporatist institutions is to give voice and levers of power to a variety and range of social interests—"stakeholders" and the "social partners" in postwar terminology—so that they might be able to have a say or even a veto in market decisions that would harm them. The individualism of free enterprise is submerged in favor of these entities and the state representing them. This purpose, or function, expresses what might be called *solidarism/communitarianism* and *consensualism/unanimitarianism*. The very word "corporatism" (*corporatavismo* in Italian) derives from *corporazione*, the Italian word for the medieval guild, which served to empower the artisans in a craft.[3] It is clear on its face that the system operates to *facilitate* the introduction of changes in the direction of the economy sought by the state, following consultations and negotiations with stakeholders and social partners, and to *impede* (thus also to discourage) or *block* changes opposed by some of the stakeholders or partners: relocations of firms, entry of new firms, and so forth. The system's performance thus depends heavily on the established roles of established companies, helped by local and national banks.[4] (The name "corporatism" fell into disuse after the second world war and was replaced by the *social market* in Germany, *concertazione* in Italy and *social democracy* in France. Yet some French politicians and journalists freely speak of *corporatisme*. In any case, the western continental European economies are still importantly corporatist, including those in the big three—Germany, France, and Italy—both in structure and in intent.[5])

Today economists view capitalism as having evolved into a rousing system for cutting-edge innovation and view corporatism as designed for industrial peace, social consensus and community stability—Mars and Venus, roughly speaking.

The thinking in the second half of the 1920s was more nearly the opposite. In 1927 Italy was suffering the effects of an exchange rate stabilization similar to Britain's crisis over its revaluation of the pound and it was at that time that Mussolini abandoned the experiment with neoclassical policies and sought the ideas for revamping the economy that would be dubbed corporatist. The redesign was to *go for growth*. Gino Severini's *futurist* paintings came to symbolize the aim of the new economic policy. The economic historian Marcello de Cecco comments on the added purpose, writing about this period, remarks:

The limits and modes of State intervention were to be established not by theory but by necessity, and the only imperative was that of making the country as rich and powerful as was possible, given the constraints that existed at all times.[6]

Yet the Italians did theorize. Many of the corporatist theoreticians thought that the corporatist system beginning to take shape in 1927 would be *more* dynamic than capitalism—maybe not more fertile in little ideas, such as might come to petit bourgeois entrepreneurs, but certainly in big ideas. Not having to fear fluid market conditions, an entrenched company could afford to develop expensive innovations based on current or developable technologies. And with industrial confederations and state mediation available, such companies could arrange to avoid costly duplication of their investments. The state for its part would promote technological advances in cooperation with industry.[7] The state could indicate new economic directions and favor some investments over others through its instrument, the big banks. In the eyes of these theoreticians, then, the system's purpose was a mobilization of the nation's collective knowledge—a view that might be termed *scientism*.

The Corporatism in Keynes

Keynes in the mid-1920s confronted an economic system in Britain that suffered many of the stresses that Mussolini's new economic policy aimed to solve. And Keynes, then in his early forties, was not too old to be intrigued by the new arguments against the Smithian economic model coming out of Italy. Keynes's political economy in fact showed some parallels with corporatist thinking. Some of these parallels are in the area of industrial organization theory and industrial policy.

Keynes an Exponent of Top-down Growth

Contrary to American impressions that his microeconomics was neoclassical—more than Marshall's was—Keynes rejected atomistic competition as an efficient market form. The policy he advocated called for the government to assist the ongoing movement toward cartels, holding companies, trade associations, pools, and others forms of monopoly power; then the government was to regulate the affected industries.[8] "In the 1920s at least," James Crotty concludes, "Keynes was unabashedly corporatist, supporting a powerful microeconomic as well as macroeconomic role for the state."[9]

Such a wave of consolidation and unionization did occur to varying degrees in the 1930s not only in the United Kingdom but also on the European continent and in the United States. In the United States by the end of the decade, there were three giant auto makers where there had been tens of companies in the early 1920s. The Temporary National Economic Committee (TNEC) was established by Congress in 1938 to advise on the regulatory and dissolution questions posed by the oligopolistic organization of much of American industry. This was the corporatist-tinged system that prevailed in the United States from the presidential terms of Franklin Roosevelt through those of Richard Nixon, whereupon it began to erode and, in places, to break up with antitrust breakups, deregulation initiatives, and global competition.

Was this modified system for the good, as Keynes and the corporatists believed? The economies of scale, Chandler's economies of scope, and the dynamic economies of "learning," or practice, on the repetitive assembly line that were achieved over the span of consolidation/rationalization (leaving aside the unionization, which may not have helped) running from 1920 to 1941 must have been extraordinary. The increase in hourly productivity and of total factor productivity over both those decades were unprecedented and have not been matched since (with the possible exception of the past ten-year span). Hitler marveled at the stunning productivity level at the Ford Motor plant, according to records of his "table talk" in the early 1940s. But was this system better at *innovating* than was the system of the 1920s that it replaced? In the judgment of Joseph Schumpeter in 1944 the answer was yes. That is also the verdict of our own William Baumol in his 2003 book.[10] But the econometric results are not in—not yet, although it is safe to say that they are now not far off. In an excoriating attack on that period, Carl Schramm sees it as having been replaced in successive steps beginning in the 1970s by a more nearly capitalist system that is far more innovative than the semi-corporatist system was.[11]

In the late 1930s and early 1940s Friedrich Hayek was to initiate a modern theory explaining how a capitalist system, if not too weighed down with imperfections and departures, would possess the greatest dynamism—not socialism and not corporatism.[12] First, virtually everyone right down to the humblest employees has arcane "know-how," some of it what Michael Polanyí called "personal knowledge" and some merely private knowledge, and out of that an idea may come that few others, if any, would have.[13] In its openness to ideas of all or most participants, the economy tends to generate a plethora of new ideas. Second, the pluralism of experience and knowledge that the financiers bring to bear in their decisions gives a wide range of entrepreneurial ideas a chance of an informed, insightful evaluation. And, importantly, the financier and the entrepreneur do not need the approval of the state or of social partners. Nor are they accountable later on to such a social body if the project goes badly, not even to the financier's investors. So projects can be undertaken that would be too opaque and uncertain for the state or social partners to endorse. Third, the pluralism of knowledge and experience that managers and consumers bring to bear in deciding which innovations to try and which of those to adopt is crucial in giving a good chance to the most promising innovations launched. Where the continental Europe system, acting in the spirit of scientism, convenes experts to set a product standard before any version is launched, capitalism gives market access to all versions—an inconvenience that pays off later.

Keynes writing in the mid-1920s knew nothing of such an argument. Keynes must have reflected upon the theorizing of the Italian corporatists and of Theodore Roosevelt's Progressive Party but could not have encountered the Hayekian argument for the superior innovativeness of capitalism. There is nothing in his writings up to that time that suggests he would have been attuned to it.

Keynes Disdainful of the Quest for Wealth

Keynes was blind to almost all of the satisfactions that might come from an economy of real dynamism. He brilliantly grasped the results of Frank Ramsey on the optimality of growing through capital formation until some sort of "bliss" level of satisfaction is reached: After all, he had inspired Ramsey to do the analysis and he provided Ramsey with an intuitive explanation of the algebraic formula for the optimum rate of saving. Keynes's *Economic Possibilities for our Granchildren* reflects in several passages his clear understanding of the benefit— mainly in the form of rising leisure—that comes from capital accumulation: from piling on more and more machinery until the marginal productivity of it has ceased to justify any more capital deepening. He appeared to see no satisfactions from the growth process.

This attitude of Keynes—unusual for an economist—was emblematic of the intellectual current in Europe at that time called *antimaterialism*. That strain in social thought was the main theme of the

"Christian corporatism" that arose on the continent in the second half of the nineteenth century: an indifference to business life and a devaluation of wealth, its accumulation and its holding. The 1893 Papal Encyclical of Leo XIII, *Rerum novarum*, is all about the higher value to be placed on life, community, and worship compared with the materialist satisfactions of, say, consuming and earning. From this point of view, the commercial economy is no more than a regrettable necessity. That view of the world was yet another strain in twentieth-century economic corporatism, which sees a conflict between employee and shareowner, between one employee and another, and between one company and another but did not see know-how, entrepreneurship, and innovation as driven by various materialist desires including the pursuit of wealth, know-how, and fame.

Keynes and the corporatists did not understand that much of the huge rise of productivity that the world was to see from 1920 onward would be traceable to new commercial products and new business methods that could only have been developed and launched in the relatively capitalist economies.[14] They also did not realize that if increased wealth, which successful innovations result in, is denigrated, that would constitute one more "minus" among the pluses and minuses of undertaking innovative projects and that such an effect would put a premature end to economic growth.

Keynes Blind to the Intellectual Satisfactions in Business Life

Corporatism did not comprehend that an economy fired by the new ideas of entrepreneurs serves to transform the workplace—in the firms developing an innovation and also in the firms dealing with the innovations. The challenges that arise in developing a new idea and in gaining its acceptance in the marketplace and the challenges to management and consumers in figuring out how and whether to adopt the latest innovation provide the workforce with high levels of mental stimulation, problem solving, and thus employee engagement and personal growth. (Note that an individual working alone cannot easily create the continual arrival of new challenges. It takes a village, better yet the whole society.)

Is there any precedent for thinking that people—virtually all people—value such stimulation, mastery, growth, discovery? The concept that they do originates in Europe. There is the classical Aristotle, who writes of the "development of talents," later the Renaissance figure Cellini, who jubilates in achievement and advancement, and the baroque writer Cervantes, who evokes vitality and challenge. By the early part of the twentieth century economists Alfred Marshall and Gunnar Myrdal write that engagement in the job is already hugely important in the advanced economies. It may be that this view, sometimes called *vitalism*, is now strongly associated with the pragmatist school founded by the American William James to which Henri Bergson in France and John Dewey in the United States belonged. The American psychologist Abraham Maslow coined "self-actualization" and John Rawls the terms "self-realization" to refer to a person's emerging mastery and unfolding scope. (Amartya Sen has referred to "expanding capabilities to do things.") These two Americans understood that most, if not all, of the attainable self-realization in modern societies can come only from career. We cannot go tilting at windmills, but we can take on the challenges of career. If a challenging career is not the main hope for self-realization, what else could be? Even to be a good mother it helps to have the experience of work outside the home.

The *solidarism* that is a part of corporatist culture militates against a life of such personal development. Although anti-materialism led to a certain devaluation of wealth, and thus also to frowning on any visible efforts at increasing the amount of observable wealth one possessed, the idea of solidarism sees it as unacceptable to move out of one's place in the community. In a solaridist society people who go to great lengths to stand out in their group or to escape their group are hated.

Alas, Keynes conveyed no sense of the role of innovation in imparting excitement and personal development to business careers. Nowhere is this clearer than in his famous passage in *Economic Possibilities of our Grandchildren*:

[I]f we look into the past, we find that the economic problem, the struggle for subsistence, always has been hitherto the primary, most pressing problem of the human race.... If the economic problem is solved, mankind will be deprived of its traditional purpose.... Thus for the first time since his creation man will be faced with his real, his permanent problem—how to use his freedom from pressing economic cares, how to occupy the leisure, which science and compound interest will have won for him, to live wisely and agreeably and well.

For many ages to come the old Adam will be so strong in us that everybody will need to do *some* work if he is to be contented.... When the accumulation of wealth is no longer of high social importance,... we shall be able to rid ourselves of many of the pseudo-moral principles which have hag-ridden us for two hundred years, by which we have exalted some of the most distasteful of human qualities into the position of the highest virtues.[15]

The most basic of these is that nowhere does Keynes recognize the wisdom of the pragmatist school—from James to Dewey to Rawls and on to Sen—that people need to exercise their minds with novel challenges—new problems to solve, new talents to develop. A mistake like that in the initial premise dooms the essay to misguided conclusions, such as the conclusion that people will learn simply to enjoy things without any effort.

But if Keynes *had* recognized that people *need* a system that throws out problems to challenge the mind and engage the spirit, he would still have gone wrong. He never saw that with the technical progress and capital deepening that he aptly postulates, an ever-increasing share of people can *afford* jobs that are stimulating and engaging. So unless the economic system is prevented from doing so, more and more jobs will be *supplied* that offer stimulation and engagement. So, were working-age people not to work or to work only a few hours a week, a great number of them would find themselves deprived of the fruit that is the special prize of the most advanced economies. The only persuasive position to take is that with steady technical progress, an increasing number of jobs will offer the change and challenge that only the predominantly capitalist economies, thanks to their dynamism, can generate.

We come then to the likely answer to what might be called the Keynes puzzle. The *puzzle* is that if we accept Keynes's psychological and economic framework, which is essentially that of Frank Ramsey, we should expect to see the workweek shrinking over the centuries to next to nothing, as Keynes made explicit, and yet we see nothing of the kind. It is a fact—notorious among some social critics—that in the United States the workweek has shrunk little if at all in recent decades. Indeed, as more and more people work in the financial industry and the legal profession, we may see the mean work week begin to reverse field and rise toward some steady state level higher than it is now. The *answer* to the puzzle is that work is *not everywhere an inferior good*. It is locally inferior at an onerous work level but not at levels so low that they would deprive of us of some of the stimulation, challenge, and personal development we can find in our careers. The fact that work has not come to an end in some Ramseyan march toward "bliss" is *strong evidence* of the fallaciousness of the Keynes–Ramsey theory of what people want and where, accordingly, societies are headed—if they haven't already got there.

The Legacy of Corporatism

Keynes's thinking nevertheless proved prophetic in a way. Most of the continental economies, including even the largest ones, though repeatedly able to catch up *technologically* with the world's "lead economies" after one or more of the latter have spurted ahead, continue to exhibit sub-par innovation, job satisfaction, and employee engagement. As a result a range of social and economic indicators, from birth rates and emigration to participation rate and unemployment, continue to signal the stultifying influence of corporatist culture and policy on the continent.

Notes

This chapter constitutes the first half of a paper presented at the conference *Keynes's General Theory after Seventy Years*, July 3–6, 2006, Santa Colomba (Siena). My thoughts here about Keynes have benefited from conversations with several scholars, including Jean-Paul Fitoussi, Roman Frydman, Axel Leijonhufvud, Robert Mundell, Joseph Stiglitz, and, among those deceased, Harry Johnson and James Tobin.

1. Many blame the "social model" for the continental Europe's relatively high unemployment and anemic participation rates, though perhaps not for the lower hourly productivity. And, empirically, employment does not appear to have suffered in the United Kingdom and Ireland despite their large welfare outlays.

2. The term *free enterprise* might convey better this Hayekian conception of capitalism, but I would rather not proliferate terminology.

3. With the rise of the market economy, these bodies were criticized as monopolistic, and in the French Revolution the D'Allarde decree abolished them, though many managed to come back.

4. A recent survey of the strains of corporative economic thought in interwar Italy is Marco E. L. Guidi, 2000, Corporative economics and the Italian tradition of economic thought, in *Storia del Pensiero Economico* 40: I. The paper is available at ⟨www.dse.unifi.it/spe/indici/numero40/guidi⟩.

5. Since the Second World War, some European countries have became less corporatist with liberalizations that have reduced the monopoly power of firms and banks (as in France). In most of Europe, however, new corporatist institutions have sprung up: Codetermination (*cogestion*, or *Mitbestimmung*) has brought "worker councils," and in Germany a union representative generally sits on the investment committee of the corporation.

breakthrough development of modern growth theory, combined with over 200 years of roughly average per capita growth, provides modern economists with an advanced understanding of long-run economic behavior and the ability to make reasonably accurate predictions. For example, Leamer (2004) shows that real GDP over nearly the last forty years has never been more than 3 percent above or below its long-run trend of about 3 percent growth. But would any economist today, even with the benefit of training in frontier growth theory, try to make serious economic projections one hundred years out? Very unlikely, but Keynes did, and did so remarkably well—in all honestly, much too well—given the available theory and the existing economic conditions when he was writing.

Keynes, as well as other leading economists of the early twentieth century, did not have sufficient theory nor a sufficient empirical record to gauge long-run economic behavior the way modern economists can. Growth theory—as we know it today—did not exist in the 1930s. There was little in the way of theory that would lead an economist of that era to confidently predict a stable steady state growth path in which output remains close to its long-run trend. The Harrod-Domar model that was developed in the 1930s predicted that market economies were unstable, with chronically high unemployment and that steady states were knife-edge propositions.

There was also little to guide an economist to confidently predict long-run changes from an empirical perspective. At the time *Economic Possibilities* was written, the United Kingdom was entering its second decade of severe depression. Real GDP per person in 1930 relative to a 1.4 percent average trend was more than 20 percent below its 1913 level, and had been close to 20 percent below trend during the entire previous decade. Moreover hours worked were 27 percent below its historical average throughout the 1920s and 1930s (see Cole and Ohanian 2002). Keynes somehow remained optimistic after more than a decade of abysmal economic performance in his own country, and with the start of the Great Depression around the rest of the world:

It is common to hear people say that the epoch of enormous economic progress...is over; that the rapid improvement in the standard of life is now going to slow down....I believe that this is a wildly mistaken interpretation of what is happening...*the economic problem* may be solved,...within a hundred years. The standard of life in progressive countries one hundred years hence will be between four and eight times as high as it is to-day.

The "economic problem," as Keynes called it, has certainly been solved for the majority of households in the "progressive countries" over the last seventy-five years, as Keynes's forecast that per capita income would advance by a factor of four to eight between 1930 and 2030 (which is an eerily accurate average growth rate of between 1.4 to 2.1 percent per capita across the industrialized countries) has indeed been realized. Moreover rapid growth over the last fifty years has made many East Asian countries rich, and by 2030, which is the end of Keynes's hundred-year horizon, there is enormous potential for much of the world's remaining population to achieve a reasonable degree of economic success. China and India, which together account for close to 40 percent of the world's population, have clearly entered the era of modern economic growth, and may double their per capita income levels by 2030.

Perhaps the only regions during the lifetimes of Keynes's "grandchildren" to remain in poverty will be Africa and the Middle East, and certainly no one in 1930 could have foreseen the enormous development impediments that these two regions face. Keynes's long-run forecasts were remarkable well beyond any reasonable expectation for success in this venture.

What factors led Keynes to make such "startling" and accurate projections? Perhaps the most important reason is that Keynes had all the makings of a superb growth theorist. *Economic Possibilities* reveals that Keynes had a sophisticated understanding of the key ingredients that would form the foundations of the modern theory of economic growth, which would not be written for thirty years: technological advances, capital accumulation, low population growth. Keynes combined these ingredients with a strong expectation of the robustness of the steady state growth path, rather than the knife-edge nature of the growth path of the Harrod Domar model that dominated growth until Solow's 1956 paper. Keynes's discussion of the transformation of the leading economies from the Malthusian era—in which there was virtually no per capita income growth—to the era of sustained economic growth, could appear in a modern growth text or journal article:

From the sixteenth century, with a cumulative crescendo after the eighteenth, the great age of science and technical inventions began.... What is the result? In spite of an enormous growth in the population of the world... the average standard of life in Europe and the United States has been raised, I think, about fourfold.... in our own lifetimes,... we may be able to perform all the operations of agriculture, mining, and manufacture with a quarter of the human effort to which we have been accustomed.

Keynes's views on long-run growth, featuring the role of labor-saving technological change and capital accumulation, are squarely in line with modern neoclassical growth theory. His insights into the process of growth are truly striking.

But there is a bit—or more than a bit—of luck contributing to Keynes's successful predictions, as he perceived the Depressions of the 1920s and 1930s as purely transitory episodes that were related to post–World War I adjustments. In contrast, recent studies of Depressions—including the UK depression that began in 1921 and that would continue until after World War II—show that these long-run episodes were the consequence of poorly designed government policies that substantially reduced steady state hours and/or productivity. From this perspective the depressions of the 1920s and 1930s should have led Keynes to have important reservations about the future long-run performance of the industrial economies. Keynes, however, dismissed the impact of these policies, and clearly considered the UK depression and the Great Depression as a transitory phenomenon that was unrelated to labor policies:

We are suffering...from the growing-pains of over-rapid changes, from the painfulness of readjustment between one economic period and another... the banking and the monetary system of the world has been preventing the rate of interest from falling as fast as equilibrium requires.

Of course, Keynes did not have the benefit of modern theory to guide his assessment. But other leading economists of the early twentieth century clearly understood the contractionary implications of the policies adopted at that time. Pigou (1927) described how the United Kingdom's protracted depression was significantly affected by government policies:

[P]artly through direct State action, and partly through the added strength given to workpeople's organizations engaged in wage bargaining by the development of unemployment insurance, wage rates have, over a significant area, been set a level which is too high...and that the very large percentage of unemployment which has prevailed during the whole of the last six years is due in considerable measure to this new factor....

More generally, Keynes held the view that government policies that significantly changed the incentives to work and save did not have any significant negative effects. In the 1940s he argued that the United

Kingdom should significantly increase the taxation of capital income and adopt a capital levy, and his views considerably influenced UK tax policies through the 1970s. During the early stages of World War II, Sir John Hicks debated Keynes about the effect of high capital income tax rates. Hicks argued that high tax rates would reduce the rate of capital accumulation and growth, to which Keynes replied, "My Dear Hicks, I scarcely imagine that individuals are as actuarially-minded as you presume they are." The view that capital accumulation was insensitive to taxes led Keynes to conclude that capital income should be taxed at nearly 100 percent during the war, and that a permanent capital levy should be adopted following the war (see Cooley and Ohanian 1997).

Keynes's failure to understand the distorting effects of government policies, and his view that economic depressions were temporary bumps on the road, were central for his very optimistic and very accurate forecast of continuing long-run economic growth. Keynes was unbelievably accurate, but some of this accuracy is for the wrong reasons. The advanced economies were ultimately able to grow because the worst government policies of the 1920s and 1930s were reformed or eliminated. The UK unemployment benefits system, which initially provided very high benefit levels indefinitely for employment tenure of as little as one day, was reformed considerably, and the capital tax rate of nearly 100 percent that was adopted in the 1940s declined to a level comparable to that in the United States by the early 1980s. And in the United States, labor policies such as the National Industrial Recovery Act and the National Labor Relations Act were either unwound by President Roosevelt during World War II or declared unconstitutional by the Supreme Court. If these policies had remained in place, the United Kingdom and the United States might be much poorer today than Keynes had predicted.

The "Perils" of Leisure: The Decline of the West?

According to Keynes, the problem of producing sufficient output was not the central difficulty facing the industrial economies. Rather, it would be dealing with the "problem" of the enormous amount of leisure that would be consumed as societies became sufficiently rich and sated with physical consumption. Keynes's view was likely influenced by the fact that hours worked per adult in the advanced countries was falling during the preceding fifty years. Thus the central issue for

Keynes was creating "solutions" for "the idle hands" of the population as economies grew increasingly wealthy. Keynes forecasts that hours worked might be around fifteen hours per week, which would reflect roughly a two-thirds decline from the existing workweek length in 1929.

Keynes does not provide any details on how he arrived at this forecast, and this raises the question of what economic theory or quantitative procedures that he used to arrive at this number. The decline is much larger than a forecast produced from simply extrapolating the historical decline in hours worked. In particular, hours worked per capita declined about 10 percent in the United States between 1889 and 1929, and this same rate of decline between 1929 and 2029 generates a further 23 percent decline, far short of the two-thirds decline predicted by Keynes.

To try to shed light on this forecast and to specifically see if Keynes was making a forecast consistent with modern growth theory, I construct a model economy and simulate it in response to technological change over the century Keynes considered. The model is presented in the appendix, and here I briefly summarize it. There is a production side of the model, featuring a standard constant-returns-to-scale production function that combines labor and capital to produce a single good that is divided between consumption and investment. The production side of the model, featuring labor-augmenting technological progress and capital accumulation, is entirely consistent with Keynes's discussion. As is standard, the capital stock depreciates at a constant rate over time. There is a constant rate of technological progress that leads to increasing wealth over time. Regarding the household side of the model, there is a representative household that values consumption of output and leisure. I make use of the observed decline in hours worked preceding 1929 to quantitatively choose the preference parameters of the model that govern the income elasticities of consumption and leisure. This will tailor the model so that it capture Keynes's expectations that leisure rises as society becomes increasingly wealthy. I will then use the model to deduce the change in hours that would occur in this model economy over the century that Keynes considered.

The solution to the model is characterized by solving a set of nonlinear equations for the endogenous variables in the model—consumption, hours worked, leisure, output, and investment—at each date from 1930 until 2030. The model is solved numerically, since a closed form solution does not exist for this model.

The model generates the observed decline in hours per adult population between 1889 and 1929, and it generates a 40 percent decline in hours worked between 1929 and 2006, and a 54 percent decline between 1929 and 2029, compared to Keynes prediction of a 67 percent decline. Thus Keynes's forecast was fairly close to that predicted by a modern growth model calibrated using the methods developed by real business cycle theorists Kydland and Prescott!

Of course, technological change increases welfare by generating higher leisure and higher consumption in this model. But Keynes held a very different view regarding the value of leisure that he based on his observations of how wealthy women spent their time, and his subjective view of the value of those activities:

> ...wives of the well-to-do classes, unfortunate women...who have been deprived by their wealth of their traditional tasks, ... are quite unable to find anything more amusing.

Keynes extrapolated these opinions more generally, and clarified his view that leisure was indeed a negative consequence of economic growth: "Yet there is no country and no people, I think, who can look forward to the age of leisure and abundance without a dread."

Keynes takes on the role of a social critic at this juncture. And as a social critic, Keynes stumbles a bit, using neither observation nor theory to guide his reasoning or his conclusions. Keynes presents no evidence or analysis to convince us that wealthy women in 1920s England were indeed "unfortunate," nor does he convince us that their leisure time is unproductive. And his presumption that leisure would continue to rise significantly over time as the world became increasingly wealthy did not occur. Hours worked in the United States and the United Kingdom are in fact higher now than they were thirty years ago, and there seems to be little concern among social scientists studying time allocation that leisure time is not highly valued among households (see Schor 1992).

It is unfair to compare Keynes's social criticism presented in a brief essay to the more detailed analyses of social issues written by others around this time, but it is nevertheless significant that the works of others who addressed similar issues using a blend of economics, sociology, and anthropology are more carefully constructed and informed by observation, and have had more impact. For example, Thorstein Veblen (1899) argued that "status" drove economic activity, and provided support for this argument through socioeconomic data taken

To capture Keynes's view, I assume the following preferences:

$$u(c) - v(h) = -(c_t - \bar{c})^2 - \eta \frac{h_t^{1+\psi}}{1+\psi}.$$

This specification generates higher leisure over time as technology grows and consumption approaches the bliss point, $\bar{c}$. The key parameters in the model that govern the change in hours worked over time are the bliss point value, the curvature parameter ψ, the scale parameter η, and the growth rate of technological progress, γ. Keynes implicitly predicted a long-run growth rate of technology ranging between 1.4 and 2.1 percent per year, so I will choose a value of γ of 1.75 percent per year that is the middle of this range. The parameter ψ governs the labor supply elasticity. I assume that the Frisch elasticity is two, which is consistent with the value of this parameter used in other applications of this model. I choose values for the bliss point ($\bar{c}$) and η so that given the rate of technological change, the model generates the observed level of hours worked in the United States in 1889 and in 1929. I choose the year 1889 as the starting date as it is the earliest year for which Kendrick (1961) constructs aggregate hours worked in the United States. The remaining parameters are β, the discount factor, and δ, the depreciation rate. These are set to standard values of 0.96, and 0.06, respectively.

Bibliography

Cass, D. 1965. Optimum growth in an aggregative model of capital accumulation. *Review of Economic Studies* 32(3): 233–40.

Cole, H., G. Mailath, and A. Postlewaite. 1992. Social norms, savings behavior, and growth. *Journal of Political Economy* 100(6): 1092–1125.

Cole, H., and L. E. Ohanian. 2002. The great U.K. depression: A puzzle and possible resolution. *Review of Economic Dynamics* 5(1): 19–44.

Cooley, T., and L. E. Ohanian. 1997. Postwar British growth and the legacy of Keynes. *Journal of Political Economy* 105(3): 439–72.

Kendrick, J. 1961. *Productivity Trends in the United States*. Princeton: Princeton University Press.

Keynes, J. M. 1930. *Economic Possibilities for our Grandchildren* (chapter 1, this volume).

Koopmans, T. 1965. On the concept of optimal economic growth. *Pontificiae Academiae Scientiarvm Scripta Varia* 28: 225–300.

Leamer, E. 2004. Datapoint. *Harvard Business Review* (October), p. 24.

Ljungqvist, L., and T. J. Sargent. 1998. The European unemployment dilemma. *Journal of Political Economy* 31(3): 514–50.

Lucas, R. 1988. On the mechanics of economic development. *Journal of Monetary Economics* 22(1): 3–22.

Ohanian, L. E., A. Raffo, and R. Rogerson. 2006. Long-term changes in labor supply and taxes: Evidence from OECD countries, 1956–2004. Discussion paper. Federal Reserve Bank of Kansas City.

Pigou, A. C. 1927. Wage policy and unemployment. *Economic Journal* 37(147): 355–68.

Prescott, E. 2004. Why do Americans work so much? *Quarterly Review, Federal Reserve Bank of Minneapolis* 28(1): 2–13.

Romer, P. 1990. Endogenous technological change. *Journal of Political Economy* 98(5, pt. 2): S71–S102.

Schor, J. 1992. *The Overworked American: The Unexpected Decline of Leisure.* New York: Basic Books.

Solow, R. 1956. A contribution to the theory of economic growth. *Quarterly Journal of Economics* 70(1): 65–94.

Swan, T. 1956. Economic growth and capital accumulation. *Economic Record* 32: 334–61.

Veblen, T. 1899. *The Theory of the Leisure Class.* London: Macmillan.

7   Spreading the Bread Thin on the Butter

Axel Leijonhufvud

The power of compound interest makes an almost irresistible mental plaything. Everyone succumbs to it once in a while. You can run it backward or forward. Backward, we find that the Dutch paid the Indians much too much in purchasing Manhattan. Keynes plays this game in tracing Britains overseas investments to the Queen's share in the depredations of Sir Francis Drake. Or you can play it forward as in the possibly apocryphal story of the mathematician attending a demography conference where everybody was lamenting the consequences of 2 percent population growth a hundred years hence. "According to my calculations;" he said, "and assuming the biblical date for Adam and Eve, I find that as of this moment the Earth is a solid ball of flesh, one light-year in diameter and expanding at the speed of light."

In running compound growth backward, we have some sense of history, however sketchy, to help us decide whether a serious point is being made or someone is pulling our leg. Playing it forward from the present is trickier. Keynes was always clear that we cannot know the future and most certainly not the distant future. The economist's notion of rational choice, even be it augmented with the actuarial calculus, is to no avail in the face of ontological ignorance. In dealing with the incalculable future, he maintained, one falls back on convention. People buy life insurance or a house on a thirty-year mortgage because it is considered the prudent thing to do.

When Keynes succumbed to the imprudent whim to speculate on the economic prospects of people two to three generations hence,[1] he bequeathed us some glimpses of his own mental conventions. It is pretty clear, for instance, that like any British patriot when the Empire still stood, he felt that Drake stole the loot "fair and square." (A more modern sensibility might worry about what a potential restitution to

3.4 percent of all consumer spending in 1930, had risen to 15.2 percent by the year 2000.[7] Medical care consumes a rapidly growing proportion of national income in most industrialized countries, and in the United States at least, rising medical and medical insurance costs pose a powerful incentive to keep working.

Idleness has not exactly become the scourge that Keynes dreaded. In predicting that people would consume so much more leisure, he forgot that it would become more costly and thus missed the substitution effect of the quadrupled return to working time. My compatriot Staffan Burenstam-Linder had it more nearly right in his *The Harried Leisure Class*.[8] The "unfortunate woman" (or her almost equally unfortunate husband) in today's United States is not very likely to have a nervous breakdown from involuntary idleness but far more likely to get it from the sheer stress of combining full-time work with the "basic need" of shuttling children around to all the organized activities that have replaced unsupervised play in the dangerously unsupervised local park.

International welfare comparisons based on per capita gross national product make no corrections for gross national costs. Deflating per capita (or average household) income by the CPI is taken to yield a corresponding real consumable income. But a sizable portion of the household's revenue is actually spent on services or activities that far from being in the nature of discretionary consumption are necessary "inputs" in order to earn that income in the first place. The second car of so many American families surely belongs in that category as does the running expenses and the time spent in commuting to work. Similarly various cost-cutting efficiencies achieved by business in recent years, while reducing the pecuniary cost to the customer, have transferred time and trouble to that same representative[9] agent also with the result that the usual real income measures overstate the welfare gain.

In addition to ordinary consumption as a motive for economic effort, Keynes recognized another class of "needs," which are "relative in the sense that we feel them only if their satisfaction... makes us feel superior to our fellows." How important this version of conspicuous consumption may be is difficult to say and Keynes in fact did not make much of it. A similar but somewhat less sordid incentive is the desire to earn the respect of one's peers, and rising real income changes the conditions under which this is to be achieved as well. Not very long ago holding a steady job, managing a home, and feeding a family would suffice to earn respect in one's community. Nowadays these things are too easily accomplished, and young people search for other goals in life and other ways to impress their peers. It would be silly to try to explain all the rapid cultural changes of our times simply in economic terms. But rising real incomes *enable* new behavior patterns that may hardly have been feasible when the pressure to meet basic needs was harsher. High rates of illegitimate births, for example, are not compatible with a society in which the nuclear family is the elemental economic organization. In strictly economic terms, the stable family is something that the high income society "can afford" to do without. The emergence of distinctive "youth cultures," more or less decoupled from older cultural traditions, is also a realization of the economic possibilities of the grandchildren of Keynes's generation. Moreover, insofar as youth culture has set the directions for the evolution of popular culture in general, it has led it in a rather different direction from Keynes's conception of how to "live wisely and agreeably and well."

People of Keynes's class and generation tended to think that economic progress would have to involve also the acculturation of the lower classes to bourgeois cultural values and a variety of educational institutions were at one time founded to aid that process. Keynes, of course, was hoping to see bourgeois culture evolve away from what it then was in a Bloomsbury direction. But he would not have envisaged the middle classes emulating ghetto tastes.

Keynes was looking forward to a time when "the problem of economic necessity" would be solved for "ever larger and larger classes and groups of people." Although he had noted that the "relative needs" might well be "insatiable," he still thought that these people would recognize that this would also change "the nature of one's duty to one's neighbour." A pious hope of an impious man! The extent to which people remain motivated by "relative needs" rather than just by real income is apparent at both ends of the real income spectrum, by the competition for status in the corporate world as well as in youth gangs. The spectacular earnings of our New Managerial Class are largely unrelated to any demonstrable marginal product or social contribution—and time in the budget of the recipients hardly allows them to consume these incomes in any other sense than in the enjoyment of relative status. But the sense of entitlement of this class is strong and, indeed, seems to have grown even stronger in recent years. In the ever more elongated upper tail of the income distribution, it is the logic of tournaments that determines the distribution of prizes, and

5. A. F. Alesina, E. L. Glaeser, and B. Sacerdote, 2005, Work and leisure in the U.S. and Europe: Why so different? Harvard Institute of Economic Research Discussion paper 2068.

6. E. C. Prescott, 2004, Why do Americans work so much more than Europeans? *Federal Reserve Bank of Minneapolis Quarterly Review* 28: 1.

7. US Department of Commerce (at note 2).

8. S. Burenstam-Linder, 1970, *The Harried Leisure Class*, New York: Columbia University Press. Of course, Burenstam-Linder drew his inspiration from G. Becker, 1965, A theory of the allocation of time, *Economic Journal* 75 (September).

9. Who has not been caught in the dungeons-and-dragons game of an automated corporate call center where the object of the game is to find a human voice at the end of the labyrinth?

10. Skidelsky notes that Keynes gave the paper in front of five different audiences between February 1928 and June 1930. He also put it in print twice. See R. Skidelsky, 1994, *John Maynard Keynes: The Economist as Savior, 1920–1937*, New York: Allen Lane, chapter 7, note 53, p. 664.

11. R. E. Lucas Jr., 2003, Macroeconomic priorities, *American Economic Review* 93: 1–14.

12. It is not clear whether this is a bow to Maynard Keynes or to Milton Friedman.

8   Economic Well-being in a Historical Context

Benjamin M. Friedman

Are we better off than our great grandparents? Do we lead happier, more satisfying lives than they did? And do we expect our great grandchildren to be happier, and more satisfied with their lives, than we are? In short, is there such a thing as human progress, and if so are we attaining it from one generation to the next?

Today most citizens of economically advanced countries would probably point first to the achievements of modern medicine. Surely we are better off—and surely it makes us happier—that fewer of our children die as infants. It likewise matters that diseases like smallpox and polio, which within living memory killed or maimed millions, are now largely under control or even eliminated. Since the discovery of penicillin and other modern-era drugs, countless infections that once were life-threatening have shrunk to the level of minor inconveniences.[1] Even cancer, in many cases, now yields to effective treatment via surgery, chemotherapy, or radiation. Here, if nowhere else, is unmistakeable evidence of progress.

Once we put advances in medicine aside, however, the claim that we are better off in some fundamental sense is harder to establish. Yes, there have been scientific advances, including expanded knowledge of the world in which we live as well as the development of countless practical applications of new technology. But few people would argue that the average citizen is happier because we now know about sub-atomic particles, or the nuclei of cells, or the age and size of the universe. Similarly, while few of us would readily give up the opportunity to travel quickly to another part of the planet, or see on television events that are taking place (or have taken place) elsewhere, or live in houses that are neither too cold in the winter nor too hot in the summer, whether our lives are really more satisfying as a result of these advantages is harder to say. Our great grandparents knew none of these developments; but were they less happy than we on that account? And will further advances that we can only perhaps imagine enable our great grandchildren to lead happier lives than ours?

Keynes apparently thought so, although the mere improvement of material living standards for their own sake was not what he had in mind. Correctly predicting that the average income in the advanced economies would continue to double every generation or two, he went on to infer that in time most citizens would be sufficiently satisfied with their material circumstances to regard "the economic problem" as "solved," and hence would be willing to devote a substantial part of the ongoing expansion of production capacity to achieving ends other than private consumption. And, here following the tradition of many utopian thinkers of the nineteenth century whose understanding of the underlying economic prospects was far less prescient than his, he further speculated that in these circumstances society as a whole would deemphasize the link between people's personal role in the production process and their claim on what gets produced, so that the typical individual would spend far less time working than in his day but would suffer no reduced access to the usual goods and services nonetheless. As a result the chief problem, as Keynes saw it—indeed, "a fearful problem for the ordinary person"—would be how to occupy the great increase in leisure time.[2]

Keynes was wrong. His expectation of a four- to eightfold increase in living standards over the hundred years from 1930 looks remarkably on target. (For America it was even too modest; extrapolation of the average increase in per capita income since Keynes wrote gives somewhat more than an eightfold gain over the hundred years.) But there is little sign of the consequences he foresaw for private consumption, for work effort, or for attitudes toward economic initiative and institutional arrangements. The source of his error—puzzling in light of his normally keen sensitivity to both the inner psychology of economic behavior and the consequences of that behavior's playing out in an inherently social setting—was his failure in this instance to bring just these insights to bear in addressing what people seek from the goods and services they consume.

Adam Smith, a century and a half before, had pointed to the unceasing quest for improvement as a central and inherent element of human nature. "[T]he desire of bettering our condition," Smith wrote, "comes with us from the womb, and never leaves us until we go into the grave. In the whole interval which separates those two moments, there is scarce perhaps a single instant in which any man is so perfectly and completely satisfied with his situation as to be without any wish of alteration or improvement." Further, economic conditions were central to the improvement that most people spent their lives seeking: "An augmentation of fortune is the means by which the greater part of men propose and wish to better their condition."[3]

Keynes expected rising living standards to cause this desire for improvement to atrophy, at least in its economic dimensions. The reason, in brief, would be satiation of people's material wants (apart from those, which he recognized but chose not to emphasize, motivated by the desire to compete with other people). An eightfold increase from what the average Brittan or American enjoyed in 1930, he thought, would be sufficient for significant satiation to take place.

But as Smith had also observed—and others beside him, including both Marx and Marshall—people's sense of what constitutes a normal everyday standard of living, and therefore what distinguishes progress from the lack of it, adapts over time to whatever their circumstances happen to be. "[A]ll men," Smith wrote, "sooner or later, accommodate themselves to whatever becomes their permanent situation."[4] Similarly Marshall noted that "after a time, new riches often lose a part of their charms. Partly this is the result of familiarity."[5] Surveys and other psychological studies have repeatedly confirmed that people's sense of satisfaction depends less on their absolute living standard, at least once it has advanced beyond some very basic level, than on how it is changing. Further, as Smith's observation suggested, even notions of what that "very basic" level is likewise appear to be highly sensitive to people's prior experience. (Even what it means to have the minimum basic nutrition is, to a surprisingly great extent, a matter of accepted habit; physical well-being improves with nutrition over a fairly wide range, but in fact people can survive with very little nutrition.[6])

The importance of improvements in living standards is likely to be especially great in just the situation that Keynes had in mind, in which technological advances are central to what makes the standard of living rise in the first place. Keynes pointed to two bases underlying the ongoing economic growth that had characterized much of the Western world since the early eighteenth century, and that he foresaw for the coming hundred years as well: capital accumulation and technological change. But when changing technology is part of the underlying process, economic growth provides people not only with higher incomes that enable them to buy more of whatever they had before but also substitutes, so that getting ahead by either benchmark strictly diminishes the urgency that people attach to getting ahead by the other one, then when everyone lives better than in the past, the effect is to diminish the importance that people attach to living better than everyone else. Hence resistance to movements that allow others to get ahead is softened, and aspirations for the public character of the society face less opposition.

Hence citizens of Britain, America, and the other economically advanced countries that Keynes had in mind are better off today because of the rise in living standards that he predicted—but simply not in the way he expected. People still seek further increases in their material living standard, and they still work hard to make that improvement happen. How to fill leisure time is not most people's problem. Nor have most of these countries sharply skewed their consumption toward public goods. But people almost surely do live in more open, tolerant, fair, and democratic societies than they would have today had there been no material gains during these seven decades. And it is a good prediction that if economic growth continues along the upper end of Keynes's predicted range, these societies will make still further progress along such lines in the future.

The same argument also applies, perhaps with even more force, in parts of the world that Keynes did not have in mind. In many countries today even the most basic qualities of any society—democracy or dictatorship, tolerance or ethic hatred and violence, widespread opportunity or economic oligarchy—remain in flux. In some countries where there is now a democracy, it is still new and therefore fragile. Because of the link between economic growth and progress in these essential aspects of political and social development, the recent strong economic performance in many countries in the developing world is welcome indeed. By contrast, the absence of growth in some of what we usually call "developing economies," even though they are not actually developing, threatens their prospects in ways that standard income and consumption measures do not begin to suggest.

Considering the implications of rising living standards for developing economies highlights the possibility, for which there is also considerable evidence, that the lines of influence between economic growth and a society's social and political structure do not run in only one direction. It does not take much knowledge of economics to realize that barring half of a country's population from receiving an education or from eligibility for certain jobs even if they are adequately educated,

simply because of their sex, is unlikely to result in the optimal deploy-
ment of the country's human resources. The same basic principle
applies to discrimination on racial or religious or ethnic lines. Research
also suggests that key institutions commonly associated with political
democracy—freedom of the press, the rule of law, and independent
judiciary review, for example—are likewise conducive of superior economic performance. Even a more equitable distribution of income,
long thought to be inimical to economic development, now appears to
be a favorable influence in this regard.[10] The idea that political and
social factors help shape a country's economic growth prospects is in
no way inconsistent with the idea that the difference between rising
and stagnating living standards powerfully affects a country's political
and social trajectory. For those countries in the developing world
where the resulting two-way interaction looks more like a vicious
circle than a virtuous one, the absence of economic growth is therefore
all the more problematic.

Even in the economically advanced countries, however—and even
with their better established and more secure democracies—some of
the same concerns are pertinent. Many countries with highly developed economies and well-established democracies, including Britain and
America, have experienced periods of economic stagnation in which
their democratic values and institutions have weakened, their commitment to a fair society with open opportunity has eroded, and intoler-
ance has gained renewed acceptance. As Alexander Gerschenkron
once observed, even a long democratic history does not necessarily im-
munize a country from becoming a "democracy without democrats."[11]

What makes such concerns especially relevant today, in many of
what are already (by today's standards) high-income countries, is the
combination of modest economic growth in the aggregate and widen-
ing inequality. In America, for example, since 2000 gross domestic
product has risen on average by 2.5 percent per annum after allowance
for rising prices. With population growth of 1.0 percent per annum,
the average increase in real per capita income has therefore been 1.5 percent. This rate of growth is within the range predicted by Keynes, though
barely; with 1.5 percent annual growth, living standards would increase
modestly more than fourfold over a century. It is certainly slower than
the average growth rate realized in the United States since 1929.

What compounds the problem of slower aggregate growth is the
ongoing trend in distribution. As in most other advanced industrialized and postindustrial economies, America in recent decades has

contribute toward preserving and even enhancing a fair and democratic society. Pursuing economic growth is the source of important
positive social and political externalities. Moreover doing so through
policies that are at the very least congruent with the characteristics of
society that we treat as central to those positive externalities—indeed,
that in many cases reinforce them—is a principle with not just conceptual but practical force. When we debate policies that either encourage
economic growth or retard it, and even when we consider our response
to growth that takes place (or not) apart from the push or pull of public
policy, we would do well to keep these potential consequences in mind.

Notes

Parts of the chapter draw on my recent book, *The Moral Consequences of Economic Growth*,
New York: Knopf, 2005.

1. David Landes opened his classic treatise, *The Wealth and Poverty of Nations*, New York:
Norton, 1998, with the vignette of Nathan Rothschild, then "probably the richest man in
the world," dying of just such an ordinary infection in 1836.

2. J. M. Keynes, 1930, *Economic Possibilities for our Grandchildren* (see chapter 1, this volume).

3. A. Smith, [1776] 1937, *The Wealth of Nations* (E. Cannan edn), New York: Random
House, pp. 324–25.

4. A. Smith, [1759] 1979, *The Theory of Moral Sentiments* (D. D. Raphael and A. L. Macfie
edn), Oxford: Clarendon Press, p. 149.

5. A. Marshall, [1898] 1961, *Principles of Economics*, vol. 1, 9th ed., London: Macmillan, p. 135.

6. See A. Sen, 1981, *Poverty and Famines: An Essay on Entitlement and Deprivation*, Oxford:
Clarendon Press, p. 12. Likewise Marx thought that people's notion of the "subsistence"
wage would likely increase over time.

7. J. S. Mill, 1907, "On Social Freedom," *Oxford and Cambridge Review* (June), p. 69.

8. John Kenneth Galbraith made this argument about the bias toward private consumption, and away from public goods, in his *The Affluent Society* (Boston: Houghton Mifflin,
1958). Contemporary economists who have prominently advanced this line of thought
include Richard Easterlin, Robert Frank, and Juliet Schor.

9. Smith, *The Wealth of Nations*, p. 81.

10. Current-day economists associated with these several lines of research on the determinants of countries' economic growth include Daron Acemoglu, Alberto Alesina, Robert Barro, Edward Glaeser, Roberto Perotti, Torsten Persson, James Robinson, Amartya
Sen, Guido Tabellini, Jeffrey Williamson, and many others.

11. A. Gerschenkron, 1943, *Bread and Democracy in Germany*, Berkeley: University of
California Press, p. 5.

12. Data are from the US Census Bureau. Data for 2006 are not yet available.

13. Data are again from the US Census Bureau.

9

Why Do We Work More Than Keynes Expected?

Richard B. Freeman

When a rich man doesn't want to work. He's a bon vivant. Yes, he's a bon vivant. But when a poor man doesn't want to work, He's a laugher, he's a lounger he's a lazier good for nothing He's a jerk!

—E. Y. Harburg and F. Saidy, "When the Idle Poor Become the Idle Rich," *Finian's Rainbow* (Broadway musical, 1947)

Pondering the increase in income per head of 2 percent or so per year in the United Kingdom and other advanced countries for a century or so, which thanks to the power of compound interest raised incomes eightfold, Keynes foresaw a future world free from economic cares. He predicted that incomes would increase massively in the next hundred years and that the higher standard of living would produce an unparalleled era of leisure, where humans would work "three hour shifts or a fifteen hour week" and "do more things for ourselves...only too glad to have small duties and tasks and routines." Keynes's grandchildren would be bon vivants not good-for-nothing jerks because they would be rich, but unlike the rich loungers of his era, whom Keynes felt "failed disastrously ... (because they had) no associations or duties or ties" the people of 2030 would lead more meaningful lives, doing a modicum of useful work as well as other morally desirable activities.[1]

Keynes was right about the rise in incomes. Compound interest at 2.1 percent per year produces a eightfold gain in incomes. As a result Keynes's grandchildren have much higher living standards than Keynes's generation: home computers, the Internet, cars, color TVs, huge medical advances, central heating (even in the United Kingdom), cheap airfare travel to anywhere in the world, and so on. But Keynes was wrong in thinking that this improvement in living standards would lead us to greatly reduce our hours and spend more time doing small household or leisure tasks. To be sure, hours worked among *employed persons* declined for much of the twentieth century but hours then stabilized toward the end of the period at levels far above the fifteen-hour work week that Keynes envisaged.[2] In every country the proportion of women working in the labor market rose greatly. In the United States the result was that between 1970 and 2005, hours worked *per adult* in the labor market increased by 10 percent while hours worked *per adult* in the household dropped.[3] A similar pattern occurred in the United Kingdom in the 1980s and 1990s. Moreover in both the United States and United Kingdom, where individuals have great leeway in choosing hours and where earnings inequality gives workers great incentive to put in long hours,[4] hours worked far exceeded hours worked in continental countries such as France or Germany, where union policies and legal institutions limit hours worked and where earnings inequality is much lower.

The United States is the most striking counterexample to Keynes's prediction that increased wealth would produce greater leisure. The United States has 30 to 40 percent higher GDP per capita than France and Germany, but employed American work 30 percent more hours over the year than employed persons in those countries. Since the United States also has a higher proportion of the adult population employed than France, Germany, and most other EU countries, the average American adult works 40 percent more over the year than the average European adult. Americans are so committed to work that they don't take four vacation days from the two weeks that they typically receive, whereas Europeans take almost all of their four to five week vacations. And more Americans than Europeans say that they want to increase hours worked than to decrease hours worked at given wage rates.[5]

The decision of Keynes's grandchildren to work so much is associated with a reversal of what had been an historic inverse relation between hours and pay. In past decades the poor have worked more than the rich. They had to work long and hard to feed themselves and their families. Work or perish. The rich, by virtue of their land holdings or hereditary position in society, could be idle if that was their fancy. The phrase idle rich had real meaning.

In the latter half the twentieth century the inverse relation between hourly pay and hours worked reversed itself, at least in the United States.[6] The workaholic rich replaced the idle rich. Those earning higher pay worked more hours than those earning lower pay. There are surely persons of great wealth who contribute nothing to the national product and persons who gain wealth through criminal work. But the typical high earner sits at the top of the earnings distribution by working a lot on something that society values. The problem for the highly paid today is not that of finding a modest amount of work to fulfil what Keynes called "the old Adam" in human nature of wanting to do something useful, but of finding ways to reduce pressures to work more. And, higher living standard or not, the problem for the low paid is to find sufficient work to earn a decent living. For the low paid it is a matter both of obtaining the money necessary to buy what have become normal consumer goods in modern society, such as televisions, washing machines, cars, cell phones, and computers, but also having a sufficient buffer in income to enable them to pay the rent, heating bills, and in the United States, medical expenses, as well as put money away for retirement, even in an economic downturn.[7]

Why did Keynes miss the boat on work?

He missed the boat by failing to appreciate the power of economic incentives to induce people, even those with high standards of living, to work long and hard. He did not expect that the increased cost of leisure due to rising wages would dominate the income effect that induces people to take more leisure. This was nothing peculiar in his expectation. Until the latter part of the twentieth century, when it became clear that people were not going to reduce hours greatly as income rose, most economists believed that the income effect was more powerful than the substitution effect. Textbooks often displayed backward-bending labor supply curves in illustrate the point. But the race between the substitution and income effects turned out to be more of a fair race than the sure-fire guaranteed winner that your local tout promised. Among women, the substitution effect due to higher wages for women dominated the income effect arising from the higher income of their spouses, leading many women to leave the household to work in the market. Among men, substitution effects greatly influenced the timing of retirements, and appear to have become dominant in decisions about hours worked, at least in conjunction with the increased inequality and tournament style economic system that gives the person who puts in an extra hour of work a potentially high return—all of which outmodes the traditional textbook representation of labor supply as a backward-bending relation.

Two other factors have enhanced the impact of the substitution effect on work. The first is the increase in inequality that was most pervasive in the United States but occurred in other advanced countries as well. Greater inequality enlarges the earnings gap between greater/lesser success in the market and thus gives workers more incentive to work long hours to succeed. Inequality, after all, involves not only a more uneven distribution of earnings, which most citizens view as undesirable, but also greater incentives to rise in the earnings distribution through hard work. If everyone is paid more or less the same, there is little pecuniary reason to put in more hours to gain a promotion or otherwise advance at work. By contrast, if pay varies greatly, there is a sizable incentive to do what it takes to climb up the earnings distribution, including putting in long hours. Empirically, advanced countries with higher inequality exhibit greater hours worked and a greater desire by the population to work more hours. In the United States, workers in occupations with high inequality work more hours than those in occupations with low inequality.[8]

The second factor enhancing the substitution effect is the rise of performance related compensation systems. Piece rate pay has declined in manufacturing due to the advent of assembly-line and team-based modes of production that make it difficult to ascertain the productivity of individual workers, but in many lines of work firms pay workers individual bonuses. Commissions are common in sales jobs. Many firms base wage increases on supervisors' evaluations of individual performance. Tournament reward systems, in which the firm promotes the best performers over their peers, are widespread. Experiments with tournament modes of pay show that increased inequality produces more effort up to point. By analogy, increased inequality may also contribute to hours worked.

Two other factors that Keynes did not foresee have also increased work time. The advent of the computer and Internet make it easier for many people to work away from their offices. In 2004, 10.2 million American workers reported that they did unpaid work at home in addition to paid work at their workplace. These workers averaged 6.8 hours of additional work—essentially an extra day for which they are not reimbursed beyond their normal pay.[9] With email and digitalization of white-collar work, it is easy to do some work-related tasks at home or after hours. The incentive for putting in the extra time is that by completing or improving projects, employees can increase their chances of being promoted or keeping their job if the firm has to lay off workers. In an economy with considerable income inequality and a low social safety net, these are sizable income incentives.

The competitive pressure that globalization places on workers also operates to induce longer hours worked. The spread of modern technology and education has created a world where low-wage workers in developing countries, most prominently China and India, are competitive with workers in advanced countries in ways that were unimaginable when Keynes wrote. Multinational firms can pressure workers in advanced countries to work longer or harder or at reduced wages because firms have an ample supply of low-wage labor in developing countries that can do much of the work. In the domestic economy, immigrants often work long hours to succeed, and immigration has been increasing rapidly even in traditional emigrant-sending European countries. Off shoring of work based on modern technology and communication further allows firms to move jobs readily to low-wage sites.

As a sign of the global pressures for workers in advanced countries to keep their nose to the grindstone, in 2006 Germany's IG Metall Union, which had been in the forefront of bargaining for reduced hours of work in the German automobile industry, agreed to extend its 29 hour work week to upward of 33 to 34 hours a week at Volkswagen without any pay rise. In return the firm committed itself to invest in German plants and to maintain production there. Absent the agreement, Volkswagen would have laid workers off and shifted production to lower wage countries.[10]

What is most surprising about Keynes's treatment of work in his essay is not his incorrect prediction that higher incomes would cause a huge drop in time worked, but his general disparagement of working overall. Using the Professor in Lewis Carroll's little known Sylvie and Bruno, Keynes mocked the purposive man who invests in the future as seeking "jam tomorrow and never jam today." He attributed this behavior to "the habits and instincts of the ordinary man, bred into him for countless generations," which creates a desire for work and an excessively low discount rate in assessing the present in terms of the future. In a world facing climate change and human destruction of the environment, the idea that people give too much weight to the future and not enough to the present in decisions seems well—misplaced, to be it mildly. Rather than mocking purposive man with the passage from Sylvie and Bruno, Keynes would have done better to pay attention to the invisible hand version of the Lobster Quadrille from Alice's Wonderland. Let me remind you of this passage, which seems apropos to the world of Keynes's grandchildren:[11]

"Will you work a little longer?" said the supervisor to the staff,
"There's a new firm close behind us doing time and a half.
Low paid foreign labor threatens to win the market race!
We must put in more hours or else we'll lose our place!
Will you, won't you, will you, won't you put in extra time?

"Will you, won't you, will you, won't you do more for your dime?

"There is another shore, you know, upon the other side.
Where the socially excluded and unemployed reside
The further off from England the nearer is to France—
It's your future, staff, unless you come and join the dance.
Will you, won't you, will you, won't you put in extra time?
Will you, won't you, will you, won't you do more for your dime?"

From the perspective of today's debates over global warming and climate change, Keynes's preference for high discount rates also strikes a peculiar chord, since it downgrades the danger that environmental change poses a major disaster to future human life. Marshall's preference for a low discount rate would seem more appropriate for a world that faces potentially catastrophic future risks, though the issue of how to evaluate such risks and the discount rate to apply is a complicated one.[12] With hindsight, Keynes's underlying postulate in his essay that humanity had effectively solved the economic problem was excessively optimistic, given the ensuing impact of economic production on the environment.

One attraction of work—the intrinsic component, which Keynes presumably viewed positively as representing higher moral value—also helps explain why his prediction of vastly reduced work hours is so far off the mark. Since work produces income, which has positive value to people, at the point where the person decides to stop working, the marginal utility of work has to be less than the marginal utility of leisure. But up to some infra-marginal point, work can be more desirable than hours of leisure, even at zero wages. Surveys that ask people about their life happiness find that unemployment is one of the major drivers of self-reported unhappiness, and one that has a larger impact than income per se.[13] Many people go to work for reasons beyond money, and might prefer to work longer than Keynes's fifteen hours a week under almost any situation. Workplaces are social settings, where people meet and interact. On the order of 40 to 60 percent of American workers have dated someone from their office. In the United Kingdom many persons look forward to the staff heading to a nearby pub at the end of the day. In the United States, and to a lesser extent in the United Kingdom, many people volunteer to work for charitable causes without pay rather than lolling around the house as did the idle rich in Keynes's era. My guess is that Keynes would applaud volunteer and charitable activities as good allocations of time, had he focused on them, but his vision of a world with no economic problems precluded some of the incentives that motivate such behavior.

In any case, we grandchildren are working far more hours than Keynes expected us to do. Perhaps we are wrong in doing this. Perhaps we should strive toward Keynes's desired outcome—a more leisurely world where people reject avarice, the pursuit of economic gain, and the rat race of work. This normative view attracts diverse social critics and analysts today, for much the same reasons that it seems to have appealed to Keynes.[14]

At the risk of being seen as a killjoy, I have the opposite view of the normative aspect of work and leisure. Rather than bemoaning purposive behavior, I applaud the internal adjustment mechanism that leads us to take today's consumption and happiness as given and to strive for improvements. As members of a thinking species on a small planet in a giant universe with no more than eighty to ninety years of life, I think it is wrong to sit on our haunches and enjoy economic well-being. We are, after all, in a great race—for life against death, for knowledge against ignorance, for exploring and understanding the world around us before the Big Contraction or Crash or whatever comes next. And hard work is the only way forward. Evolution presumably imbued us with a work ethic for our survival and not for a Garden of Eden existence. That is fine with me.

Keynes ended his essay by telling us that we ought not overestimate the importance of the economic problem in the face of "other matters of greater and more permanent significance," without specifying those "other matters." He hoped that as economic scarcity diminished economists would become humble, competent people, on a level with dentists. Dentistry? Talk about dismal professions. My hope for us and for our grandchildren is quite different. If by working hard and devising new incentive and market forms and advancing our understanding of economic behavior, economists can get ourselves thought of as visionary creative social scientists, on a level with entrepreneurs or science fiction writers or jazz musicians, that would be splendid! And if we can't be that cool, I'd rather be a sociologist than a dentist.

In short, thank heavens Keynes was wrong about the strength of human devotion to work. There is so much to learn and produce and improve that we should not spend more than a dribble of time living as if we were in Eden. Grandchildren, keep trucking.

Notes

1. J. M. Keynes, 1930, *Economic Possibilities for our Grandchildren* (see chapter 1, this volume).

2. In 2005 hours per week in the United States averaged 34.7 while those in Germany, which had one of the lowest hours worked, averaged 27.6 hours. Calculated from annual hours worked from *OECD Employment Outlook 2006*, table F.

3. Between 1970 and 2005 US hours worked per worker fell by 1 percent, but the employment rate rose by 12 percent. So hours per adult went up by about 11 percent. Data from *OECD Employment Outlook 2006* and *Employment Outlook 1985*.

4. Higher inequality in earnings creates an incentive to work long hours whenever the additional hours worked increases an individual's chance of being promoted and thus rising in the highly unequal wage distribution or maintaining employment during a period of layoffs. See L. A. Bell and R. B. Freeman, 2001, The incentive for working hard: Explaining hours worked differences in the US and Germany, *Labour Economics*, 8(2): 181–202.

5. R. Freeman, 2007, *America Works: The exceptional labor market*, New York: Russell Sage, ch. 4.

6. C. Juhn, K. M. Murphy, and R. H. Topel, 1991, Why has the natural rate of unemployment increased over time? *Brookings Papers on Economic Activity* 1991(2): 75–142.

7. For an analysis of what poverty means in a high-income country with only a limited welfare state, see M. Federman, T. I. Garner, K. Short, W. B. Cutter IV, J. Kiely, D. Levine, D. McDough, and M. McMillen, 1996, What does it mean to be poor in America? *Monthly Labor Review* 119(5).

8. L. Bell and R. Freeman, 2001, Working hard, in G. Wong and G. Picot, eds., *Working Time in Comparative Perspective*, Kalamazoo, MI: Upjohn Institute.

9. US Bureau of Labor Statistics, *Work at Home in 2004* USDL 05-1768, September 22, 2005, ⟨http://www.bls.gov/news.release/homey.nr0.htm⟩.

10. ⟨http://www.politicalgateway.com/news/read/39278⟩.

11. Adapted from Lewis Carroll by the invisible hand.

12. See William Nordhaus, 2006, The Stern Review on the economics of climate change, NBER working paper 12741, December. See also Martin Weitzman, 2007, Structural uncertainty and the value of statistical life in the economics of catastrophic climate change, NBER working paper 13490, October.

13. A. Clark and A. J. Oswald, 1994, Unhappiness and unemployment, *Economic Journal* 104(2): 648–59.

14. J. Rifkin, 1996, *End of Work* (New York: Tarcher Putnam), argued for a new allocation of time. J. Schor, 1992, *The Overworked American: The Unexpected Decline of Leisure* (New York: Basic Books), also favors a Keynesian allocation of time.

10

Context Is More Important Than Keynes Realized

Robert H. Frank

The standard of living in the United States, as measured by GDP per capita, has increased more than fortyfold since the end of the eighteenth century. In his 1930 essay, *Economic Possibilities for our Grandchildren*, John Maynard Keynes joined a large group of distinguished thinkers who have predicted that people would experience great difficulty filling their days once productivity increases eliminated the necessity to spend more than a token amount of time working. These fears seem unfounded, even comical, in retrospect. Productivity has continued rising sharply, sure enough, yet people are still working just as hard as ever.

Keynes was, by all accounts, an extremely brilliant man. But this specific prediction struck me as so absurd that I was eager to see the details of how he defended it. My expectation was that upon reading his essay, I would discover that he had mysteriously failed to take into account the boundlessness of human desire. I was thus astonished to encounter the following passage in which he acknowledged this possibility only to dismiss it:

Now it is true that the needs of human beings may seem to be insatiable. But they fall into two classes—those needs which are absolute in the sense that we feel them whatever the situation of our fellow human beings may be, and those which are relative in the sense that we feel them only if their satisfaction lifts us above, makes us feel superior to, our fellows. Needs of the second class, those which satisfy the desire for superiority, may indeed be insatiable; for the higher the general level, the higher still are they. But this is not so true of the absolute needs—a point may soon be reached, much sooner perhaps than we are all of us aware of, when these needs are satisfied in the sense that we prefer to devote our further energies to non-economic purposes.

But although Keynes was clearly aware that certain kinds of demands might continue escalating without limit, in this passage he embraced far too narrow a view of the extent to which context shapes demand. From the quoted passage, he seems to have believed that context mattered only for goods that "lift us above," or "make us feel superior to, our fellows." Like most other economists, he believed that demands originating in such feelings are at most a minor component of overall economic activity. I share that belief. Indeed few people are consciously aware of any desire to outdo their friends and neighbors. But the ways in which context shapes demand run far beyond such feelings.

The specific source of Keynes's error first became clear to me during a conversation before a lecture I gave at the University of Chicago several years ago. Three of us were waiting outside a restaurant when the fourth member of our dinner party arrived at the wheel of a brand new Lexus sedan. Once we were seated at our table, the Lexus owner's first words to me were that he didn't know or care what kinds of cars his neighbors and colleagues drove. As it turned out, I had had numerous conversations with this gentleman over the years and found his statement completely credible.

I asked him why he had chosen the Lexus over the much cheaper, but equally reliable, Toyota sedan from the same manufacturer. He responded that it was the car's quality that had attracted him—things like the look and feel of its interior materials, the sound its doors made on closing, and so on. He mentioned with special pride that the car's engine was so quiet and vibration-free that the owner's manual posted warnings in red letters against attempting to start the car while its engine was already running.

I then asked him what car he had been driving before trading up. I forget what he said, but for the sake of discussion will suppose that it was a five-year-old Saab. I asked him how he thought people would have reacted to his Saab if it were possible to transport it back to the year 1935 in a time capsule. He answered without hesitation that anyone from that era would have been extremely impressed. The car's acceleration and handling would have felt spectacular; its interior materials would have amazed people; and its engine would have seemed unbelievably quiet and vibration-free. His own evaluations of his former car were of course strikingly different on each dimension.

We then discussed what a formal mathematical model of the demand for quality might look like, quickly agreeing that any reasonable one would incorporate an explicit comparison of the car's features with the corresponding features of other cars in the same local environment.

Cars whose features scored positively in such comparisons would be seen as having high quality, for which consumers would be willing to pay a premium.

Such a model would be essentially identical to one based on a desire not to own quality for its own sake but rather to outdo, or avoid being outdone by, one's friends and neighbors. Yet the subjective impressions conveyed by these two descriptions could hardly be more different. To demand quality for its own sake is to be a discerning buyer. But to wish to outdo one's friends and neighbors is to be a boor, a social moron. To be sure, there are people whose aim is to flaunt their superiority over others. But most of us do our best to avoid such people, and the fact that we succeed most of the time suggests that they are relatively rare. My point is that by placing the desire to outdo others at the heart of his description of the category of goods whose demands are shaped by context, Keynes confined that category to the periphery.

But the demand for quality is simply not limited in this way. It applies to virtually every good, including basic goods like food. When a couple goes out to dinner for their anniversary, for example, the thought of feeling superior to their friends and neighbors probably never enters their minds. Their goal is just to share a memorable meal. But a memorable meal is a quintessentially relative concept. It is one that stands out from other meals.

Can anyone really doubt that the standards that define a memorable meal are highly elastic? When my wife and I were living in Paris a few years ago, we went out to dinner with well-to-do friends who were visiting from the United States. The restaurant we chose had a good reputation and, by our standards, was not cheap. My wife and I enjoyed our meals enormously. But it was clear that our friends found theirs disappointing. I'm confident that they were not trying to impress us or make us feel inferior. By virtue of their substantially higher income, they had simply grown accustomed to a higher standard of cuisine.

There are no obvious limits on the extent to which quality standards can escalate, since the richer we become, the more we are willing and able to pay for memorable experiences. Even if you choose the least expensive wine on the list, dinner for two at Sketch in London can easily top $700. For that price, you'll get a memorable meal. But productivity will continue growing, and it is just a matter of time before the price of a memorable meal becomes twice that amount. As our incomes rise, chefs will discover novel ingredients and new ways of combining them with traditional ones into ever more interesting and exciting meals.

As we approach the frontiers of existing quality standards, even minor quality improvements can be enormously expensive. Until recently, for example, the Porsche 911 Turbo was considered perhaps the best all around sports car that money could buy. Priced at over $150,000 with even minimal options, it handles impeccably and completes the standard zero-to-sixty sprint in a blistering 3.9 seconds. But in 2004 Porsche raised the bar with its new Carrera GT, which handles slightly better than the Turbo and beats its zero-to-sixty time by two-tenths of a second. People who really care about cars find these small improvements genuinely exciting. To get them, however, Carrera GT buyers must pay almost three times as much as for the 911 Turbo.

Quality standards have escalated sharply even for bicycles, the simplest form of transportation other than walking. The lighter a bicycle is, the better. But manufacturers have long since exhausted the cheap and easy ways of making bikes lighter. The Serotta Ottrott frame, hand-built from carbon fiber and titanium, sells for $5,300. People who care enough to buy that frame will also want wheels with carbon-fiber rims, steel spokes, and aluminum hubs ($2,500 a pair); carbon-fiber forks ($600); and Shimano Dura-Ace brakes, derailleur, crankset, cables and shifters ($3,000). Add a seat post, seat, headset, pedals, and a custom paint job and you have a bike that sells for $14,210. For the moment, it's a bike that any enthusiast would love to ride, even someone who didn't care at all about feeling superior to others. But at some point soon, it, too, will seem out of date.

I am laboring the point, because it is an important one. The demand for quality is universal and inexhaustible. Keynes and others were thus profoundly mistaken to have imagined that a two-hour workweek might someday enable most people to buy everything they ever wanted. That will never happen.

Keynes did, however, make one other specific prediction in his essay that has proved strikingly on target, at least in some countries. Thus, he wrote, "I see us free, therefore, to return to some of the most sure and certain principles of religion and traditional virtue... that those walk most truly in the paths of virtue and sane wisdom who take least thought for the morrow." Here, Keynes envisioned a day in which living standards would be so high that people would no longer feel compelled to accumulate additional capital. In the United States that

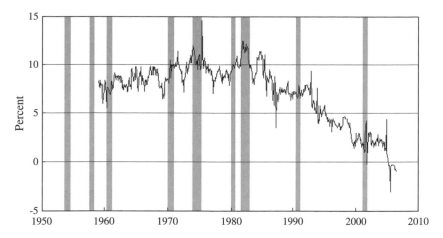

Figure 10.1
Personal savings rate in the United States: Personal savings rate (PSAVERT).
Shaded areas indicate recessions as determined by the NBER, 2006, Federal Reserve Bank
of St. Louis (*research.stlouisfed.org*). Source: US Department of Commerce: Bureau of Economic Analysis.

prediction has been realized with a vengeance—although not for the reasons he imagined.

Thus, as shown in figure 10.1, the American personal savings rate began a steady decline in the mid-1980s and actually became negative in 2005, the first time that has happened for an entire calendar year since the Great Depression. This decline does not appear to have resulted from Keynes's prediction that the desire for additional consumption goods would eventually be sated. On the contrary, our debt levels and bankruptcy filings now stand at record levels, and when we take more time off from work, it is only when legislation either requires or encourages us to do so.

The decline in personal savings rates is especially puzzling in light of the fact that income and wealth inequality have been rising sharply in the United States in recent decades. Although the reigning permanent income and life-cycle theories of savings claim that the rich save at the same rate as the poor, people who actually work with the data have long since conceded James Duesenberry's point that the rich save at much higher rates. So if most of the income gains in recent decades have been accruing to top earners, it would seem that aggregate savings rates should have been rising, not falling.

Here, too, a possible reconciliation of the apparent contradiction is suggested by the influence of context on demand. Evidence suggests that spending by the wealthy has little direct effect on the consumption context that shapes spending by middle-income consumers. For people at all income levels, what matters most are the expenditures of others with similar incomes. And data suggest that no matter how we sub-divide the population, we see a similar pattern of increased inequality.

Thus, in each group, most income growth is confined to the top quintile of earners, with little significant income growth experienced by others.[1] For example, this pattern is observed for college graduates, engineers, dentists, and real estate agents. The pattern also repeats itself as we move up the income ladder. Among the top quintile of earners, for instance, the lion's share of all income growth has been captured by the top 1 percent. Among the top 1 percent, similarly, most of the income growth has gone to the top one-tenth of 1 percent.

The upshot is that during the last several decades, most consumers' incomes have failed to keep pace with those of people at the top of their respective personal reference groups. Within each group, increased incomes of top earners have led those people to spend more, which in turn appears to have induced other members of the group to have spent more as well, even though their incomes have not grown signifi-cantly.[2] In short, even though we are richer now, on average, the local contexts in which we operate have also shifted. In relative terms most of us, even the very rich, are poorer than in the past, and hence per-haps our declining savings rate.

Keynes, of course, was hardly the only economist to have ignored the central role of context in shaping demands. Indeed neoclassical models continue to assume that utility depends only on the absolute amount of consumption in each category. These models completely ignore any possible role of context.

Failure to incorporate the influence of context is responsible not only for prediction errors of the sort that Keynes and others have made but also for even more important errors in welfare analysis. Conventional invisible hand theorems say that efficient allocations result when peo-ple decide individually how to spend their incomes in unfettered mar-kets. But if context shapes demand more heavily for some goods than others, these theorems no longer hold. Conventional models that incor-porate context portray welfare-reducing distortions analogous to those we see in military arms races.

The essential idea can be grasped easily by asking yourself which of the following two worlds you would choose if you were society's me-dian earner:

A: You save enough to support a comfortable standard of living in retirement, but your children attend a school whose students score in the twentieth percentile on standardized tests in reading and math, or **B:** You save too little to support a comfortable standard of living in retirement, but your children attend a school whose students score in the fiftieth percentile on those tests.

Because the concept of a "good" school is inescapably relative, this thought experiment captures an essential element of the savings decision confronting most middle-income families. In most jurisdictions, after all, school quality is strongly correlated with the average price of houses in the corresponding neighborhoods. There are perhaps no expenditure categories for which context is more important than those that can ensure that our children will enter adulthood successfully. And buying a house in a safe neighborhood with good schools is perhaps the most important such expenditure.

If others bid for houses in better school districts, failure to do likewise will often consign one's children to inferior schools. Yet no matter how much each family spends, half of all children must attend schools in the bottom half. The choice posed by the thought experiment is one that most parents would prefer to avoid. But when forced to choose, most say they would pick the second option.

Of course, saving less today means having to endure a lower standard in retirement. But even though context surely matters for the evaluation of future consumption, most parents would be willing to tolerate reduced living standards in retirement if that meant being able to provide a better environment for their children today.

When the extent to which context shapes demand differs across domains, the general result is that expenditure shifts in favor of the domains most sensitive to context, reducing aggregate welfare in the process. As noted, this claim is precisely analogous to the claim that closely matched rival nations tend to spend too much on military armaments. A necessary and sufficient condition for the latter claim is that relative position matters more for armaments than for other goods—a condition that surely holds in practice. Being less well armed than rivals puts a nation's political independence at risk. And although the utility from consumption of nonmilitary goods may also depend on the corresponding levels of consumption in other countries, the consequences of having fewer toasters and televisions are much less severe than the consequences of being less well armed.

In the private consumption arena, credible evidence suggests that the sensitivity of demand to context differs sharply across multiple domains.[3] Demands for leisure and safety, for example, are far less sensitive to context than consumption demands generally, which is consistent with the observation that most societies take collective steps to promote both leisure and workplace safety. Yet despite the existence of norms, laws, and regulations that stimulate consumption of goods whose demands are least sensitive to context, substantial welfare losses remain. Elsewhere I have described how switching to a steeply progressive consumption tax would boost savings and help eliminate welfare losses of several hundred billions of dollars a year or more in the United States alone. This claim has been energetically contested.[4] Yet the premises on which it rests are completely uncontroversial.[5]

What is perfectly clear, in any event, is that Keynes needn't have fretted about the possibility that our grandchildren might someday feel hard pressed to fill their days. The economic challenge, as he called it, will always be with us. Local context shapes perceptions of quality, the demand for which knows no limits.

Economic historians will someday struggle to explain how the profession could have ignored the seemingly obvious influence of context for so long. The key to explaining this anomaly is that Keynes, like most other economists, understood this influence far too narrowly.

Notes

I thank Lorenzo Pecchi and Gustavo Piga for helpful comments on an earlier draft of this chapter.

1. See R. H. Frank and P. J. Cook, 1995, *The Winner-Take-All Society*, New York: The Free Press.

2. For evidence of inequality's role in this process, see R. H. Frank and A. S. Levine, 2006, Expenditure cascades, mimeo, Johnson School, Cornell University.

3. See R. H. Frank, 1999, *Luxury Fever*, New York: Free Press.

4. For example, A. Kashdan and D. Klein challenge this claim in their 2006 paper Assume the positional: Comment on Robert Frank, *Econ Journal Watch* 3(3): 412–34 ⟨http://www.econjournalwatch.org/pdf/KashdanKleinCommentSeptember2006.pdf⟩.

5. See, for example, R. H. Frank, 2006, Taking libertarian concerns seriously: Response to Kashdan and Klein, *Econ Journal Watch* 3(3): 435–51 ⟨http://www.econjournalwatch.org/⟩.

11   The End of (Economic) History

Jean-Paul Fitoussi

Some papers, for reasons that remain at least partially obscure, leave a persistent trace in intellectual history. Such is the case with Keynes's *Economic Possibilities for our Grandchildren*, although it never attracted much attention within the economic profession, besides reference here and there to the power of simple economic calculations: "The greatest economists of my lifetime have been extraordinarily wise in guessing by rule of thumb what the more elaborate models of the cliometricians will derive after tedious calculation" (Samuelson 1983). A possible explanation is that Keynes, in freeing himself from economic rigor, is attempting to unveil his moral philosophy. There is nothing wrong in such an attempt as it is utterly normal that a thinker of the caliber of Keynes undertakes to look beyond his own field. Because a great economist is not necessarily a great philosopher we should not ab initio expect the result to be at the level we are accustomed to in reading Keynes. But we should nevertheless expect it to be worthwhile, as what matters is not so much the way Keynes answers the questions he poses but the nature of the questions themselves. Could the very functioning of the capitalist system lead to the solution of the economic problem and hence to the end of capitalism itself? Would an era of abundance entail a radical change in the system of values on which capitalism presently relies? What can the life of the people in the new era reasonably expected to resemble?

The answers by Keynes to these questions are grounded on three elements: arithmetic, the neurosis of capitalism, and the communism of the elites.

Arithmetic

At the beginning of Keynes's reflection is the calculus of compound interest and its well-known spectacular outcome when applied to long

periods of time. At a rate of growth of 2 percent any figure will be multiplied by 7.5 in a century. So would be the GDP per capita of human
beings living in the civilized world, thanks to capital accumulation
and technical progress.[1] Keynes is prudent enough to give a multiplier
lying in between 4 and 8. With insight backed by powerful intuition, a
back-of-the-envelope calculation may deliver more truth than the most
sophisticated model. That is the most robust element of Keynes's paper. One could quarrel with the mercantilist view of capital accumulation developed in the paper or with its explicit focus on developed
"progressive" countries—Europe and the United States. But even if he
would have taken into account the developing countries, Keynes's prediction would not have been that wrong, thanks to China, India, Brazil,
and the like, before 2029 which is the time horizon of the reasoning.

So what? Would the economic problem of humankind be resolved
by an eightfold increase of all economic dimensions but the population? The answer by Keynes is a straightforward yes, because such an
increase will allow the satiation of what he calls "the absolute needs."

True, Keynes is well aware that relative needs—keeping up with the
Joneses—will never be satiated, but he thought that to the extent that
the needs of the first type would be satisfied, those of the second type
would become of a second order of importance. Implicitly, he thinks
that the rush to fulfil the desire for superiority will appear so remote
from the search for the good life that it will soon be recognized as a
mental disease rather than a sign of strength. Indeed Keynes is refer-
ring to the nervous breakdown "which is already common enough in
England and the United States amongst the wives of the well-to-do
classes, unfortunate women, many of them who have been deprived
by their wealth of their traditional tasks and occupation . . . ." Of course,
Keynes was not predicting that in one century from now we should
expect a general "nervous breakdown" because "mankind will be
deprived of its traditional purpose." We would progressively learn
how "to devote our further energies to non-economic purpose."

But here sheer arithmetic should have rung a bell in Keynes's ears:
nowhere in the paper is Keynes concerned with income distribution,
nor is he expressing the idea that inequalities will progressively, if not
disappear, at least significantly shrink. Now an eightfold increase of all
percentiles of the income distribution leads to an eightfold increase
in the absolute differences between the percentiles. Relativities stay
unchanged, but the range of the distribution is becoming so huge that
it will make people of the same society live in entirely different planets.

In the 1920s inequalities were considerable, perhaps as considerable as in the belle époque. Keynes was well aware of that state of affairs in other texts; as in *The General Theory*, he considered income and wealth inequalities as one of the two flaws of our system, the other being unemployment. But in *Economic Possibilities* he disregards completely the question as the following quotation of the paper shows: "Let us, for the sake of argument, suppose that a hundred years hence we are all of us, on the average, eight times better off in the economic sense than we are to-day." Now even if the utility function of every household is of a lexicographic type, we are not sure that an eightfold increase in its income will allow it to satisfy its absolute needs.

Here ends arithmetic and begins the complexity of human nature. How can we define "absolute needs"? Like Marx, by the value of the goods necessary for the reproduction of the workforce of a wage earner? Or by what Ricardo calls the subsistence level of wage? Are absolute needs independent of time and place? Were they the same at the beginning of the twentieth century and are they now? Answers to these questions are crucial to Keynes's thesis. A straightforward yes would mean that he is right, a no that we are in trouble. And I think we are in trouble: a human being is a social being, and this has far-reaching consequences. One of them is on the definition of "absolute needs." If we depart from the fiction that economic agents are Robinson Crusoes, we have to define absolute needs as those whose satisfaction allow social inclusion, and not, as Keynes does, those "that we feel whatever the situation of our fellows human beings may be." But that means that absolute needs are relative after all! They are relative even if we do not take account of social interaction: life expectancy has increased with time thanks to the progress of medicine and hygiene and to the increased quality and diversity of the basket of goods aimed at satisfying the "absolute needs." They are relative because there is no such a thing as a one-to-one mapping of specific goods to each "absolute need." They are relative because at a certain date and place, goods are more or less satisfying the needs to which they apply: think of glasses, water, bathroom heating system, medicine, prostheses, beds, and the like. The demand for a better match between goods and needs seems to be boundless and constitutes one of the more powerful engines for scientific research and innovation—in short, progress. The taxonomy of needs between absolute and relative is too crude to serve as a hierarchy for human wants. Even if we limit ourselves to the fulfilment of subsistence needs, we have to admit that the degree with which goods may satisfy those needs may vary widely with the quality of the goods (e.g., think of the complementarity between goods' quality and health). Hence the positional concern of consumers is not the only sign of nonsatiation of needs; the search for a better life suffices.

Why does a brilliant's mind like Keynes rely so heavily on such a simplistic characterization of human needs? One possible answer is that he uses it as a rhetoric devise to belabor his point "that the economic problem is not—if we look into the future—the permanent problem of the human race." For all of us who believe in economic and social progress, this statement may be exaggerated, but not entirely wrong. There is little doubt, if we learn how to avoid the potential catastrophes emerging from our time and mode of development—such as climatic change, wars—that economic and social progress will in a remote future lead to the resolution of the most pressing economic problems on a global scale. At least we could hope that a time will come when the economic problem will no more be as it is today, a question of life and death. I am writing these lines from France, a very rich country where each week brings its news of the death of some homeless person. But the social protest against homelessness is very strong, and all political parties have agreed to sign a charter to put an end to such a state of affairs. There also exist in France "restaurants of the heart," privately funded establishments that serve millions of lunches and dinners to the needy, and their number has been increasing year to year since the early 1980s. Indeed it is feasible to believe that essential needs will be satisfied in a not so remote future. To become reality, this utopia needs at least two conditions, an increase of the standard of living through compound interest, and social cohesion, that is the refusal by members of society to endanger the life of the poorest through a lack of redistribution. But that will not mean that the economic problem will be solved, rather that its nature will change. There is no such a thing as a stationary state, where with all needs being satiated, humankind will cease to hope for a better future, at least on earth.

Another complementary interpretation is that Keynes is trying to oppose a "modern" view to the grand (but melancholy long-run) dynamics of the classics. Keynes seems to be addressing Ricardo, Malthus, and Mill.[2] They were the theorists who set the stage for Carlyle to call economics "the dismal science" with the specter of stagnation as the inevitable long-run fate of economic prophecy, mainly due to diminishing returns. In *Economic Possibilities* Keynes is extolling the virtues of increasing returns, hence his affinity with Solow, Lucas, and compound interest. After all, if increasing returns and compound interests trees can, so to speak, grow sky high—the end of scarcity—and the avarice of Nature as emphasized by the classics is no longer a limiting factor.

But the emphatic tone Keynes is using throughout the essay aims at a more definitive conclusion: that of the solution of the economic problem. He has to believe in his own taxonomy of needs to reach such a conclusion. How could it be? A possible explanation lies with his understanding of Freud's contribution. According to Skidelsky, "Keynes was fascinated by Freud's reflection on the pathology of money, particularly its association with the anal sadistic character, and by the Freudian mechanism of sublimation. Freud enabled him to build on his insight into the sacrificial nature of capitalism, first expressed in Keynes's *The Economic Consequences of the Peace*. Here the price of economic progress is seen as the cultural deformation of the 'rentier bourgeoisie' who have sacrificed the 'art of enjoyment' to 'compound interest.'" The "love of money" that Keynes seems to associate with the satisfaction of relative needs is thus indicative of a neurotic disposition, and in a world where all the material needs are satisfied, the course toward differentiation would appear inadequate so as to be remote from the good life. Keynes is drawing on pathological cases for some general conclusions. Psychoanalysis is teaching that human desire cannot be satiated because of a permanent, boundless human search for fulfillment. Of course, desire and needs are not the same thing. But it can easily be imagined how the boundlessness of desires translates into the boundlessness of needs.

The Unlovable but Unavoidable Capitalism

Pathological cases aside, Keynes nevertheless expects a prosperity whereby it is "in the long run that mankind is solving its economic problem."[3] Of course, the road to prosperity is never smooth, but those who are intelligent enough would discern under the surface "the trend of things." So the time will come when economic history will end. This is the message Keynes wanted to convey to his readers in prophesizing the withering away of the problem of economic scarcity. The illusion of the end of history has re-emerged recently in Francis Fukuyama's thesis. For Keynes it is the end of the struggle for subsistence that leads to the end of (economic) history. For Fukuyama, it is the end of the struggle between ideologies and the triumph of liberal democracy that leads to the end of history, *tout court*. It is interesting to notice that both conclusions are consequences of a dichotomy—between absolute and relative needs in Keynes's essay, and between Soviet socialism and liberal democracy in Fukuyama's book. The prophecy of the end of history seems hence to be the outcome of a narrow, partial vision of the world. But here the similarities end. In Fukuyama's view, it is the satisfaction of the need for recognition by liberal democracy that provides the end point for history. In contrast, the need for recognition would rather be classified by Keynes within the range of relative needs. Hence on this point their conclusions are incompatible.

Furthermore there was a period when the feelings of Keynes about Soviet socialism were ambiguous. In the article he published upon his return from Russia in the October 25, 1925, issue of *The Nation* ("Soviet Russia"), he even asserted: "It is here [Russia] that we feel from time to time, despite poverty, stupidity and oppression, that lies the true laboratory of life." Indeed most of the arguments of *Economic Possibilities* are already contained in this article.

What Keynes disliked most about capitalism is that economic means are an end in themselves, but he found Soviet socialism to be even more detestable both as a political and an economic method. Hence if capitalism is taken as an efficient means—however disgusting it may sound—and the advent of pure communism as the only moral end of any economic system, compound interest will lead to that end. In other words, there are at least two ways to reach abundance, through Soviet socialism and through capitalism. While the former explicitly moves in that direction—in promising after a period of transition the advent of pure communism in a world of abundance—the infringement of freedom was not something Keynes was ready to accept: "Comfort and habits let us ready to forgo, but I am not ready for a creed which does not care how much it destroys the liberty and security of daily life, which uses deliberately the weapons of persecution, destruction and international strife" (Keynes 1925, p. 258). Capitalism is thus to Keynes the surer way, and although he does not find much to recommend to it, its efficiency as a method to increase the standard of living was proved in past centuries. Capitalism might be morally inferior, because of less attractive human behavior and because vices are confused with virtues, but in Keynes's new era "we shall be able to rid ourselves of many of the pseudomoral principles which have hag-ridden us for two hundred years, by which we have exalted some of the most distasteful of human qualities into the position of the highest virtues. The love of money as a possession.... will be recognised for what it is, a somewhat disgusting morbidity, one of those semi-criminal, semi-pathological propensities which one hands over with a shudder to the specialists in mental disease."

One cannot but agree with Keynes's view that economic progress should serve moral objectives and yet disagree with the caricatured picture he gives of capitalism. If avarice, the exaction of usury, the love of money were the main characteristics of capitalism, certainly the system would not be efficient and able to deliver, even several centuries ahead, the fruits of abundance. If purposiveness has always to be considered a vice, investment, education, and entrepreneurship would have to be considered sins. Whatever the world in which we live, it would be hard to understand why carpe diem is always morally superior to the action we must undertake in consideration of tomorrow and even the day after tomorrow. It may even be that the moral strength of capitalism is its consequentialism as it can lead to intergenerational altruism. As Edmund Phelps forcefully argued in his Nobel Lecture, a good economy—via entrepreneurial capitalism—may even deliver a good life.

Elite Communism

Any articulated proposition can be considered a metaphor, combining the idiosyncratic circumstances in which we live, the fashionable ideas of our time, our moral judgments about the social framework, and a vision of the world that we dream will prevail—dream, not hope as sometimes we do not want our dreams to come true. Then we have to recognize that Keynes's *Economic Possibilities* contains all these elements of a metaphor.

This is why, depending on the angle from which his essay is viewed, his thinking may appear sophisticated or simplistic, as almost right or exactly wrong. In particular, Keynes's calculation is almost right, his rejection of capitalism—because of the greediness it exacts from economic agents and their egoistic behavior—is not so badly founded. But there are many moral principles, and the one Keynes seems to prefer is not so superior indeed! It is a pity to find in a paper so great a contempt for so many categories of people: the purposeful, the Jews, the wealthy classes, the wives of the well-to-do classes, and so forth. "Yet it will be only for those who have to do with the singing that life will be tolerable and how few of us can sing!... But it will be those peoples who can keep alive, and cultivate into a fuller perfection, the art of life itself and do not sell themselves for the means of life, who will be able to enjoy the abundance when it comes." This kind of arrogance is all but sympathetic; it is so idiosyncratic of Keynes's milieu, so remote from the virtues he seems to praise that it is no wonder that it did not pass the proof of time.

The "educated bourgeoisie," those who had been at Eton and frequented the Bloomsbury circle, are those who are elected to the new paradise after the end of economic history. They had the luck of benefiting from the then luxury goods, higher education, an understanding and appreciation of the arts and music, and so on, because they had the means to pay for these pursuits and the leisure time to enjoy them. The others, "the ordinary persons with no special talents," will have to elevate themselves in order to benefit from the new freedom they are entitled to. The first, rather than the last, will, on the contrary, be chosen to enjoy this paradise. Keynes here, somewhat naively, nods to Freudian sublimation. Only those who are able to sublimate their non-satiated relative needs to a higher ideal can find their way to paradise. "We shall honour those who can teach us how to pluck the hour and the day virtuously and well, the delightful people who are capable of taking direct enjoyment in things, the lilies of the field who toil not, neither do they spin."

Elite communism may appear to be a contradictory phrase, but Keynes's wording does not allow for any other interpretation. Of course, with time and in a world of abundance one might expect the class of elites to become larger. But such enlargement could well lead to Schumpeter's prediction as interpreted by Samuelson: "That rationality of Capitalism which makes for productivity will serve to corrode the irrational sentiments of social cohesiveness. The spoiled children of affluence will reject their parents and heritage. Their self-hate will lead to boredom and anomie." I prefer, without hesitation, the conclusion of Keynes that an increase in the standard of living will help cure us of our neurosis over that of Schumpeter according to which it will aggravate it. It is not pure chance that capitalism, with its built-in Keynesian mechanisms—a system that Schumpeter calls capitalism under an "oxygen tent"—has been a success story since the end of World War II, which even Lucas (2003) recognizes.

But I do not understand Keynes's position when he asserts that we should value ends above means. First, it appears to contradict Keynes's own rejection of socialism: he finds the Soviet regime detestable as a means but not its end, which seemed to him to contain the germ of an ideal ("Soviet Russia"). Second, and more important, such a principle is morally highly questionable. The caricatured Machiavellian principle according to which the ends justify the means has led in the past to the most abominable, atrocious actions of mankind and today it helps to justify terrorism and torture. It is why, already for a long time, it has been consensually agreed at least in the democratic countries of the world to obey the Gandhian principle that on the contrary the ends do not justify the means. One can attempt a generous interpretation of Keynes's assertion, according to which he wanted to alert the reader on a possible confusion between ends and means. After all, such confusion is very common nowadays, so common that it frequently leads to an inversion in the hierarchy of socioeconomic objectives (a lower level of public debt rather than a higher level of employment; a balanced trade account rather than a higher level of growth, etc.). But it is difficult to believe that a thinker of Keynes's caliber does not pay attention to the words he uses, especially in the final version of a paper that he had already presented several times.

I end this reflection with mixed feelings. What is remarkable in "the economic possibilities" is the powerful intuition of Keynes and even more remarkable the nature of the questions he poses. Each and every economist should try to answer the question of the ends of the economic system and of its possible end. Maybe this would lead them to consider their discipline differently. What is deceptive is the naivety with which Keynes deals with human needs and even more deceptive his arrogance and the questionable moral that goes with it. Of course, I know that Keynes condemned Nazism as early as 1933, but I know also that for reasons that pertained to an exactly inverse perspective than that of "the economic possibilities"—the short-medium run rather than the long term—his preface to the German edition of *The General Theory* was very ambiguous vis-à-vis the German regime.

Notes

The quotations are from *The Economic Possibilities for our Grandchildren* unless otherwise specified. I am very much indebted to Vela Velupillai for helpful comments on earlier versions of this chapter.

1. Ever since, the power of compound interest has always amazed economists. As Lucas wrote: "in Korea, over the same period [1960–1988], per capita income grew at 6.2 percent per year, a rate consistent with the doubling of living standards every 11 years." And Lucas concluded: "If we understand the process of economic growth . . . we ought to

be capable of demonstrating this knowledge by creating it in these pen and paper (and computer-equipped) laboratories of ours. If we know what an economic miracle is, we ought to be able to make one." (Lucas 1993) Utopias are alive and well!

2. This interpretation has been suggested to me by Vela Velupillai.

3. In *The Tract on Monetary Reform*, Keynes told us that we were all dead in the long run! He should have added that fortunately for humankind our grandchildren will be alive!

Bibliography

Fukuyama, F. 1992. *The End of History and the Last Man*. New York: Free Press.

Keynes, J. M. 1925. Soviet Russia. *The Nation and Athenaeum*, October 10, 17, and 24. Reprinted in *The Collected Writings of John Maynard Keynes*, vol. 9. London: Macmillan, pp. 253–71.

Lucas, R. J. 1993. Making a miracle. *Econometrica* 61(2): 251–72.

Lucas, R. J. 2003. Macroeconomic priorities. *American Economic Review* 93(1): 1–14.

Phelps, E. S. 2006. Macroeconomics for a modern economy. Nobel lecture, Stockholm University, December 8.

Samuelson, P. A. 1983. The world economy at century's end. In S. Tsuru, ed., *Human Resources Employment and Development*. Vol. 1: *The Issues*. London: Macmillan.

Skidelsky, R. 1992. *John Maynard Keynes*. Vol 2: *The Economist as Saviour*. London: Macmillan.

12

All the Interesting Questions, Almost All the Wrong Reasons

Michele Boldrin and David K. Levine

Here is the bottom line: Keynes got his economic theory wrong, and the facts too. But, and not a minor feat, he got all his questions and his guess about the future right. This may prove that while the man was a tad arrogant, he perhaps was not a fool. Perhaps, indeed, he was brilliant, possibly so much so that he never had to bother with logical consistency and facts adequate to convince his audiences that he had got it right. That is a pity, because he could have spared humanity a whole lot of poor economic advising, and academic economists a never-ending debate about what he "really meant," had he bothered to ponder a bit longer upon some of his statements and their analytical underpinnings. Bygones are bygones, and the questions he posed are among the most important an economist may dare to ask. Let us begin with the questions, continue with Keynes's answers, and then figure out why, despite guessing it right, he got all the "reasons" wrong.

The Questions

1. Is the 1930s "attack of economic pessimism" due to permanent and fatal causes, or is it just a transitory one?

2. Until the recent depression got underway, we had been growing at unprecedented speed for the last couple of centuries or so: where did such growth come from?

3. Roughly until AD 1700 humanity's standard of living had barely moved since the neolithic age: Why did economic stagnation last so long and characterize all societies earlier than ours?

4. What, if anything, does our understanding of the causes of economic growth so far suggest about our foreseeable economic future?

The Guesses

1. The malaise is temporary, and will go away. It may be partly accidental, due to mistakes the banking system has made in not letting the rate of interest fall quickly enough, but its main cause is the exceptional economic growth of the last few decades, which was in turn due to major labor saving technological changes. This has led to a fast reduction in the demand for labor while the pace at which we were capable of finding new uses for it has been much slower, hence the high *technological unemployment* we currently experience.

2. Historical experience shows that the sources of economic growth are capital accumulation by compound interest, and science cum technical invention. The kickoff was a sudden accumulation of financial wealth—mostly stolen gold—that was wisely invested abroad and that, by compound interest, grew to unexpected amounts.

3. The sources of stagnation, first, and, later, of depression have been, respectively, the unexplained failure of every society prior to the British one in AD 1700 to engage in both technical progress and capital accumulation, and the natural inability of most humans to find something useful to do with the excess time that technical progress frees from work.

4. The future can bring us more of this bounty if we steer the ship away from (a) the storms of war and civil disorder, (b) the sand banks of lack of trust in scientific invention, (c) the contrary winds of population growth and, (d) the gorges of investment falling below saving. As the latter—hear it, hear it—tends to adjust by itself as long as the previous three are satisfied, the long-run outlook is basically good. The standard of living a century hence will be between four and eight times higher than today.

All right, he got carried away a bit with his claim of "humanity solving its economic problem" and England reaching a per capita income eight times as high as the one in the 1930s, but more than three times is still a pretty good achievement! More to the point, Keynes got his main prediction right. The 1930s depression, even the Great Depression of the United States, was a temporary event that has not repeated since; technological progresses and capital accumulation have continued—in the so-called progressive countries and in the few more that joined the club—at an unprecedented speed. Finally, our standard of living is already between four (USA) and almost eight (Japan) times what it was back in the 1930s, with twenty-four years to go on Keynes's clock. The man had a superb intuition, an unflinching trust in the capitalistic system, and a hardly matched ability for seeing straight and clear into the long-run trends of our societies, even in the long run in which he, at least, is dead.

He asked the right questions, and he also made almost all the correct predictions. But, we insist, he incoherently answered the underlying *economic questions*: he guessed the correct outcome, but his guesses hardly followed from the analytical apparatus he set up, or the historical facts, or plain logic. In other words, as our title insists, he suggested all the wrong *reasons* for his correct guesses. Because, as an economist and a thinker rather than as a guru looking into a crystal ball, Keynes was highly respected and listened to, it is the analytical apparatus he used and the economic logic with which it was instilled that matter. It is Keynes's economic theory and method that have survived almost to our day and affected generations of economists and policy makers around the globe, not his lucky predictions about growth continuing at around 2 or 3 percent a year for the century after him.

Let us be clear. That fact is the only one he got right; from that follows the rest of his predictions. Even during those years of widespread gloom he was not, however, the only optimist, and his trust in the capitalist system, while possibly fading in the intellectual circles he spent most of his life within, was not particularly unique in the world at large. It was Keynes's analytical apparatus that left a permanent mark on the pathways of economic science, not his lucky guess, and it is in this sense that, here like elsewhere, he got most of his "reasons" wrong. To see why, we better forget the guesses for a while, and focus on the internal structure of his arguments and his readings of the facts.

The Answers: Keynes's Model of Economic Growth

1. Technological change leads to labor-saving innovation.

2. This leads to unemployment: because, first, the freed labor supply does not meet a compensating demand from other sources, and second, humans are naturally programmed to work long hours. Hence humans cannot adapt quickly to using their free time in activities other than working and producing.

3. Unemployment can be eliminated if either additional demand for consumption goods emerges or humans develop an interest in leisure

and activities other than economic ones. This requires even longer time and more adaptation than coming up with new consumption needs.

4. There is a tension between two sides of the human soul, or even two kinds of humans: the wealth-seekers and those that pursue the art of life through leisurely activities. The first side (or kind) will produce, accumulate wealth, and make us richer until a state of abundance and satiation is achieved. At that point the other side (or kind) will take over, and we will all be working little, if at all, and enjoying the arts during most of the day.

The closing lines read like the description of realized communism in Karl Marx, when machines will produce everything, everyone will be able to consume according to "his needs" and poetry writing will rule; but never mind. That also Keynes could let his imagination fly free and come up with utopian descriptions of the far away and ideal future society is not something either strange or surprising. Equally unsurprising is his (and Karl Marx's) failure to anticipate how technological progress might not only satisfy existing wants, but create new ones. What we are concerned with here is the internal analytic structure of each one of these steps and, in particular, with the light they may shed on Keynes's better known and still widely believed theories about economic policy and the functioning of the competitive market system.

Can Labor-saving Innovations Cause a Depression?

No one doubts that labor-saving technological change can lead to sustained growth in productivity and income per capita. The question then is, how does this happen and is the manner in which labor-saving innovations are adopted bound to lead to long-lasting periods of economic depression, as Keynes claims in step 2?

What evidence did Keynes have to support the statement that technological progress caused the depression that England, and a number of Western economies, experienced in the 1930s? As far as we can tell, none. Growth in England from 1913 to 1930 was not high—in fact income per capita did not grow during this period but instead fell off just a little bit (Cole and Ohanian 2002)—and, what is more important, growth was much lower than during the decades preceding WWI or in the six decades after the end of WWII. The growth of labor productivity, in particular, slowed down progressively both in England and in the rest of Europe, while it continued at roughly the same pace in the

United States, until 1929. Had Keynes got it right, the great depression should have taken place in the United States only: in Europe the labor-saving innovations he had in mind dated about thirty years before the time of his writing. So we must conclude either that the depression could hardly qualify as "temporary" or that Keynes had not bothered to look at the data.

Looking at the data would have lead him to realize, among other things, that while all the inventions he listed had been adopted by most European countries, Australia, Canada, Japan, and the United States, growth dynamics were uneven across the same set of countries. During the two decades preceding 1930, labor and total factor productivity growth in the United Kingdom was slow, not booming, and it was turning negative right at the moment of Keynes's writing. Japan was showing no signs of depression and was in fact beginning a substantial acceleration. France was growing briskly but would enter a long recession the following year, the same one in which, instead, Australia escaped its own. There is no space for a more detailed examination of the facts, but all the studies we are aware of (e.g., Cole and Ohanian 2002; Crafts 1999; David and Wright 1999; Gordon 2004, 2005) show that evidence suggesting the Depression was due to an extraordinary wave of labor-saving inventions is altogether absent.

If the facts militate solidly against Keynes's statement, maybe some economic theory supports his model. Having worked ourselves on the theoretical side of the issue (Boldrin and Levine 2002, 2006), we can certainly think of labor-saving innovations as generating subsequent growth in productivity and income, accompanied by an asymmetric U-shaped path for employment. Maybe the latter is what Keynes had in mind: there is no doubt that a labor-saving innovation initially decreases employment for given output. That is, after all, how it is defined, despite recently popular "Keynesian" econometric research claiming that a positive technological shock cannot induce a short-run reduction in employment (Gali 1999, and the literature following it) because the identification procedure defines a "technology shock" as the one that raises employment asymptotically. There is little doubt, though, that even if employment does drop initially it will recover after the innovation is introduced, as more of the technological improved capacity is added and growth resumes briskly. In this case it is the speed at which new productive capacity is accumulated that determines the growth rate of employment, and there is little, either in the theory or in the evidence, suggesting that a twenty-year-long depression would normally ensue, unless the innovations being considered were of a magnitude we have not yet faced.

Pause for a moment, and take stock of one finding: that long-run growth comes from *factor-saving, and particularly labor-saving, innovation* is a coherent hypothesis, supported by theory and a substantive amount of statistical and historical evidence. While this may sound obvious to most students of actual economic growth, it is not according to recent theoretical trends. Hence we use this opportunity to lay bare the essential argument.

Labor-saving innovations can be modeled as either exogenous or endogenous. Trivially everything is endogenous, but it is sometime useful to treat technological progress as exogenous. This is what Robert Solow (1956, 1957), among others, did about fifty years ago, and we have no complaints about that choice: given the state of knowledge and the issue addressed, that was the right way to proceed. Exogenous labor-saving technological progress needs to be Harrod-neutral or labor-augmenting in order to be reconciled, if ever vaguely, with long-run data. In such a case it certainly cannot cause any form of unemployment or even a reduction of employment. Other versions are certainly possible, for example, Hicks-neutral, but they all lead to one kind of complication or another. Nothing against complications here, some of them are useful and stimulate original thinking. The fact is that among all the interesting complications we know of, a reduction of employment has not yet been found to be the consequence of an exogenous increase in labor productivity—unless, we should add, one believes that the income effect dominates the substitution effect. In that case, though, employment decreases not because there is less demand for it but because less of it is supplied by the now richer households. This is not what Keynes had in mind: his concern is that such an income effect is not strong enough and that people want to work too much instead of taking the leisure they ought to, given their newly acquired productivity and wealth. Summing up: while Keynes might have guessed right that labor-saving innovations are the engine of economic progress, there is no coherent sense in which their exogenous version can generate the technological unemployment he talks about.

Conceive, then, of labor-saving innovations as endogenous. Details of the model aside, when a costly innovation is adopted (free innovations will always be undertaken, hence they are tantamount to exogenous ones), there must be some convenience in so doing. Because a labor-saving innovation reduces labor demand for given amounts of output and all other inputs, its cost must be compensated by the implied reduction in the wage bill. Hence such innovations will be more frequent the higher is the real wage, everything else equal. When innovations of this kind are undertaken by many firms, the aggregate demand for labor drops, and in the presence of an upward-sloping supply of labor, this cannot lead to an increase in the real wage, at least immediately after the new technology is adopted. Could this induce a long-lasting drop in employment? This question is answered negatively in the model we have proposed, but we can conceive of other situations where it may happen, which gives hope of modeling coherently what Keynes argued. Two cases stands out as particularly relevant, and are better understood against the background of our preferred parable of labor-saving innovations and growth.

After the innovation is undertaken, demand for labor drops, and so does employment. Because the wage bill per unit of output is now lower than before, there is an incentive for profit-seeking capitalists to invest in the new technology—an exogenous reduction in the real rate of interest may help, but is not required in what follows. Capitalists invest in the new kind of productive capacity, which increases the demand for labor. This leads to an expansion with increasing labor productivity, wages, and output per capita. The expansion comes to an end when productive capacity of the new kind is so large that labor has become too costly to allow further profitable investment. At this juncture either the economy reaches a new steady state (with higher income, wages, and labor productivity) or a new innovation is found that is profitable, and the virtuous cycle of growth repeats itself. In this story there is no depression but a temporary drop in employment, the asymmetric U-shaped pattern of employment mentioned earlier. Was this Keynes's model? We like to think it is, as it would allow us to enroll in the ever-powerful army of "Keynesianism" and feel part of a larger intellectual community than the one we are currently enlisted in. Unfortunately, everything Keynes wrote conflicts with this, personally desirable, conclusion. Nevertheless, if this is what "Keynes really meant," then we were "Keynesian" from the start, and did not know.

Back to the cases where a permanent reduction in employment can be engineered, then. There are two cases we can think of. One assumes that building productive capacity of the new kind is very costly and therefore proceeds slowly. When accumulation proceeds slowly, low employment may persist, possibly for a long while. Maybe this is what Keynes had in mind, as his reference to the interest rate not having dropped to the new equilibrium would suggest, when interpreted loosely. But this gives us a coherent theory only on the account of pretending that "moody entrepreneurs" are the main driving force behind economic growth, and here is why. If accumulating new capital is very costly, this may be because it actually is so on the ground of fundamental facts or because those that are supposed to purchase it believe it is so on the ground that they are in a period of low spirit and have little desire for more capital. In either case, reducing the rate of interest may seem helpful. Helpful, though, in what sense?

Begin with the case where capital is not being accumulated because entrepreneurs do not find it convenient, and this is due to a correct evaluation of the costs and benefits of new enterprises. Consider first the case of a temporary reduction in the rate of interest. This would be of no great use in the circumstances considered. Investment projects last for more than one period and are irreversible, which is particularly the case when productive capacity incorporating new technologies is being built. A temporary drop in the real rate of interest may induce a temporary jump in the investment rate only if the investment game is over after one period. If instead the new productive capacity is expected to last for more than one period, while investors know that the drop in the real rate is only temporary, nothing will happen. Entrepreneurs will reason: once the new capacity is installed and the desired rate of return on capital goes back to its original higher level, those undertakings that appeared profitable, when the rate of interest was low, will start making losses and be terminated, together with the employment they had only temporarily produced.

Move next to the case where entrepreneurs are in a bad mood and their "animal spirits" make them pessimistic about the future, even if there is no good reason for them to be so unhappy. If entrepreneurs are in low spirit, then offering them a temporarily cheap price of capital may cheer them up, get investment started again, allowing the price of capital to rise back to the permanent equilibrium level if the joyfulness continues. Indeed even a reduction in the short-term interest rate might cheer them up. Perhaps so too would a circus.

On the other hand, how can one lower the desired rate of return on capital forever? Lowering the rate of interest permanently is clearly useful both when entrepreneurs are "rational fundamentalists" and when they are "spirited animals," so consider how this may be achieved. Certainly not by convincing the bankers as Keynes seems to imply, since bankers are also profit maximizers and we do not expect them to lower their prices just to do theorists a favor. They may be "surprised" into it, as we had been taught for many decades, but this, as the 2006 Nobel Prize winner taught us, does not really lead very far and certainly does not lead to a permanent reduction in the real rate of interest. Increasing saving permanently would do it in fact: it seems to be pretty much the only way in which a permanent reduction in the rate of interest can be engineered. Walking through this door, though, leads us into a complicated world we have not yet well mastered: how do we change the propensity to save and invest forever? This requires a change in preferences of a kind opposite to the one Keynes advocates—it requires a generalized increase in thriftiness, avarice, and parsimony—so let us leave it at that for now.

The second road to persistent lower employment following a labor-saving innovation is more "Keynesian" in spirit: rigid (real) wages. If the drop in labor demand caused by the innovation is not accompanied by a reduction in wages, the accumulation of capital, caused by the initial labor-saving innovation in our parable, will be slower. Still it will not lead to a permanent reduction in employment, just to slower growth and faster adoption of yet another labor-saving innovation. If it were profitable to employ one worker at a wage of one apple to produce two apples before the innovation cut the labor input in half, it should be profitable to employ (at least) the same worker at the same wage to produce four apples after the innovation is introduced. Unless, clearly, the cost of innovating exceeds the additional two apples produced by that one worker with the new machine. In that case the labor-saving innovation would have never been adopted in the first instance, and the story is over before it starts. This suggests one extreme possibility: following the adoption of the innovation, the drop in the demand for labor induces a sharp increase in the real wage rate, an increase large enough to cancel out the beneficial effects of technological progress. The outcome is a state of higher output, productivity, and wages but lower employment. In a world with trade unions and all kinds of labor market imperfections, this is certainly a possibility and one that a number of European countries appear to have experimented with, on and off, since the early 1970s. Maybe Keynes had conceived of "Eurosclerosis" almost fifty years before it materialized, a fascinating conjecture indeed. Nevertheless, again, this is not what his writing suggests: there is no trace of an excessively high real wage in the article, nor does he seems to be blaming unions and other market rigidities for keeping the wage too high and impeding employment growth as, instead, recent literature seems to be convinced was the case (Cole and Ohanian 2002). He blames, briefly, the interest rate for being too high, and as we already saw, this road does not lead to the desired implications.

Conclusion: all the facts we are aware of suggest that Keynes did not bother to check them before making his statement that labor-saving innovations caused the malaise, and there is no coherent economic model of labor-saving technological progress, be it exogenous or endogenous, that predicts a persistent employment depression of the kind the United Kingdom, and the United States, experienced during the 1930s—unless, as we insist, Keynes had in mind supermonopolistic labor unions raising real wages in the face of declining employment. Maybe this was the case, but then should not our author have told us so, instead of spending various pages debating the sociopsychology of effective demand failure?

The Sociopsychology of Effective Demand Failure

Let us move forward and consider the second half of point 2 and point 3 in Keynes's putative model. This allows us a glimpse of the sociopsychological foundations of Keynes's most famous "contribution" (quotations marks are *de rigueur*, as you will see) to economics: the theory of effective demand failure. Here are the key phrases in the light of which the whole text should be interpreted:

We are being afflicted with a new disease of which some readers may not yet have heard the name, but of which they will hear a great deal in the years to come—namely, *technological unemployment*. This means unemployment due to our discovery of means of economising the use of labor outrunning the pace at which we can find new uses for labour.

The analytical potential of this most captivating overture we have already examined, and it leads to the theoretical hypothesis, considered earlier and there discarded, according to which Keynes was assuming that either wages were too high or new investment too costly to keep up with the unusual pace at which innovations were shaving labor away. But this is not what he had in mind because, once the paper progresses, it is on another kind of theory that he focuses that is beautifully summarized by the words:

Yet it will only be for those who have to do with the singing that life will be tolerable and how few of us can sing!

This is Keynes's main concern here: the brutish part of ourselves, or the brutish ones among us (the many who cannot sing), still want to work and accumulate instead of taking up music. May we advance the absolutely crazy idea that here rest the microeconomic foundations of Keynes's theory of aggregate demand failure?

We have been taught in school that Keynes is the man that first clearly figured out why the market mechanism is not self-equilibrating, why Say's (or was it Walras's?) law does not hold, and why economic crises and depressions are intrinsic and unavoidable features of a market economy. When we were taught classical Keynesian economics—that is long before the recent explosion of post, new, and neo-Keynesians variations appeared—the logic was relatively straightforward. Wages and prices are rigid (that is both the main assumption and a self-evident truth) and human desires and plans are volatile, while installed capacity and the size of the workforce are not. Because of this, demand for goods and services oscillates wildly, following the equally wild movements in animal spirits. The good times come when demand is high, so that plants can run at full capacity and the workforce be fully employed, but in those ugly days or months in which the population is, for whatever reason, depressed and pessimistic, demand is low, and because of price rigidity, lots of productive capacity, both physical and human, goes unemployed. This situation we call one of "lack of effective demand," and it is due to the self-evident failure of free markets to bring about the necessary changes in the relative prices of goods and factors.

Well maybe, but this is not the impression one garners from reading this particular piece. Why? First off, he never mentions any of these factors: no rigid wages, no animal spirits, no demand for investment incapable of equilibrating with its supply, that is saving. Second, he explicitly denies such possibility when he states that "... and the rate of accumulation as fixed by the margin between our production and our consumption; of which the last will easily look after itself, given the first three."

We read the latter as saying that markets will do their job, and saving will equal investment, as long as "the first three" conditions mentioned earlier are satisfied. No failure of capitalism and free markets here, just the opposite. Still, Keynes argues, we cannot currently find uses for the excess labor that technological progress has generated, and this is due to (1) approximate satiation of our material needs and (2) an animal-like impulse to work, work, work. We will spare you the irony of having to consider the mass unemployment of the depression as due to a primitive desire to work even if it would have not been necessary per se. We will not do this; still we will insist on our un-orthodox thesis that this whole paper and, most important, the discussion about the lifestyle of the aristocratic people

[who have] return[ed] to some of the most sure and certain principles of religion and traditional virtue—that avarice is a vice, that the exaction of usury is a misdemeanour, and the love of money is detestable, that those walk most truly in the paths of virtue and sane wisdom who take least thought for the morrow.

has to be read as Keynes's microfoundations of the theory of effective demand failure. The following constitutes indeed the biological under-pinnings of the "animal spirits" concept, ordained to become the theo-retical jack-of-all-trade of Keynesian economics: humans are mostly brutish animals, biologically selected to work and greedily seek satis-faction of a few basic needs. When such needs are satiated, humans will still want to work and accumulate (as workers and capitalists, re-spectively), but (as consumers) they will be unable to dream up things to demand and new material wants to satisfy. Being satiated, they can-not generate additional demand; being brutish, they seek to generate additional supply. Notice that the unpredictable and altogether arbi-trary "animal spirits" are not needed here to make the theory coherent. Some of the people, or a part of people's brain, having reached sati-ation is no longer increasing its demand for produced goods and services, while some other people, or the other portion of the brain, in-satiably wants to work, produce, and accumulate: hence the effective demand failure, hence the need to repeatedly engineer persistent drops in the real rate of interest, to artificially induce demand for goods where there would not otherwise be, waiting for the humans to evolve out of their satiated and brutish schizophrenia. Like it or not, this is the least inconsistent sociopsychological foundation of the theory of effec-tive demand failure we are aware of. Once its aristocratic overtones have been stripped away, it may even have something to do with very recent research in decision theory, as we speculate at the end.

The bio-cultural theory of human preferences Keynes proposes, and we are now stepping into the territory of point 4 in Keynes's hypothetical model of economic growth, is also a beautiful exercise in stretched coherence. There are two kinds of needs, we are taught: the absolute and the relative. The first satisfy the satiation assumption, while the second do not as their value is determined in a kind of habit-forming or catching-up with the Joneses' fashion. Good, one says, as long as preferences are insatiable along some dimension: economic growth, even if it needs effective demand to be spurred, will continue along those dimensions. But the relief is short-lived as the "relative needs" do not seem to have an economic nature: we (well, only some of us) actually like to devote our energies to noneconomic purposes, we are told. What a "noneconomic purpose" is that nevertheless requires expense of human energy, it is not clear and it is never said. What is said is that it is somewhat "nonhuman" as the whole species has been nurtured for solving the economic problem. Why a machine that has been built for the exclusive purpose of doing A will suddenly elect to do $-A$ even when it does not know how to do $-A$ and, as a consequence, has a nervous breakdown, we are again not told.

Let us stop here. The point is not to be facetious but to underline a mode of reasoning that is completely unscientific. In the light of contemporary moral values, obviously Keynes's statements read as utterly classist, sexist, and eurocentric—just notice how he ignores the economic conditions of about 6/7 of humanity that, especially at the time of his writing, no one could possibly assume capable of overcoming the economic problem within a century. Leave these issues aside; the man was after all a man of his time. What is really surprising is that one could try to build a theory, economic or not, of the long-run evolution of humanity on such a badly assorted collection of British upper-class prejudices: the sloppy description of human preferences we just ridiculed, the completely unsubstantiated argument about the existence of two kinds of humans, the neurotic housewifes, the vulgar rich person, the lazy but artistically inclined rentier....

There is hope nevertheless even for the masses of nongeniuses: a little amount of work will apparently be available even in the country of unbounded cornucopia we are fast approaching, and these few hours of work may be enough to keep the inferior among us away from the psychiatric ward while those who can sing will reproduce and spread around, and maybe educate the least brutish among the other humans. Once the transformation process is completed, effective demand failures will forever be gone, and central bankers with them. There is always a silver lining.

Keynes's View of Human History and of the Origins of Growth

In 1930 the love for wealth and money, apparently, was only about 200 years old, and bound to disappear into eternal oblivion about a hundred years hence. Never mind that today, only twenty-four years from the end of history as we have known it, you do not yet feel the symptoms and that, apparently, about three billions of Chinese and Indians are going crazy for accumulating wealth and material goods. That much even Keynes was not able to forecast, he was not Karl Marx after all. What is truly amusing, though, is the fact that such a finely educated superior being as Keynes had never heard of the Fuggers and the Medicis, of the Roman senators and the Pharaohs, of the Shylocks, and the Gengis Khans. In fact he had not even heard of the (Christian) Church and of the Jews, as the first had been prohibiting interest (simple or compound, equal sin) for more than a millenium—evidently someone had been sinning—and the second had been sinfully delegated to take care of collecting it.

No doubt Keynes was right that he lived in a period of unsurpassed technological and economic wealth and continuing transformation. As we talk today of "jobs being exported overseas" so then Keynes worried neurotically about too many workers becoming redundant due to technological change—despite, as we have remarked above, ample evidence that this does not happen, and that it was not happening at the time.

For Keynes history starts about three hundred and fifty years before, roughly in 1580. Before that time, certainly for four thousand years, nothing happened—and this was because of the lack of technological progress and the failure to accumulate capital. Then the Industrial Revolution struck and everything changed. If Keynes is to be believed, in 1000 BC we already had banking, the state, religion, astronomy, and mathematics, they have apparently not changed or improved since, and, indeed, nothing else worth mentioning had been invented by humans until about AD 1700. We will leave aside the fact that, as an empirical matter, this is as false and simplistic as anything can be (Diamond 1997; Lane 1963; McNeill 1963; Mokyr 1990; Rostovzev 1926; Trevor 2000), since, unfortunately, Keynes is not alone in perpetuating this myth that has made it almost intact to contemporary writers of economic growth. Taking up in the remaining three pages the whole "nothing happened 'till the Industrial Revolution" narrative is not feasible. So let us focus on a couple of minor, but revealing, points of theory.

What is truly fascinating is how confused Keynes was between real and monetary factors, between aggregate accumulation and private and nominal accounting profits. Accumulation, he say, begins in the sixteenth century and was driven by the price inflation spurred by the arrival of Spanish gold and silver from the Latin America colonies. Such inflation generates profits, we are told. How this could be—how inflation can generate real physical surplus—only Keynes knows. For every borrower who profits as the real value of his debt collapses, is there not a lender who looses his shirt?

Nay, assume someone makes profits and this is all that matters, maybe because those making the losses do not count or disappear. Forget also the fact that the "inflation" of that period is partly due to fast population growth during a long respite from the plague and it corresponds, as historians have well documented, to a decrease in the average standard of living. Maybe the inflation, by making borrowers richer, transferred resources from an incompetent and primitive social class (the lenders) to a trade-oriented, capitalist, and entrepreneurial one (the borrowers), and this got that great thing called the Industrial Revolution going. Forget the obvious fact that this had happened dozen of times before in Byzantium and Venice, in Florence and Maastricht, in the Flanders and Cadiz, in Hamburg and Marseille, and still the Industrial Revolution had not come.

Forget all this obvious common sense, and just ask: who were the big borrowers of Europe during the sixteenth century? The autocratic kings, obviously! Like Henry VIII, who debased the currency around 1542 to get (partially) out of his troubled debt position (this is the century of Gresham, after all, later to become an advisor to Elizabeth I). Or Felipe II, of Spain, the most eternally in debt of them all. If this is not enough evidence to convince anyone that Keynes's theory of the causes of the Industrial Revolution was just a made-up-on-the-spot story meant to impress the audience until he left the room in the midst of applauses, nothing else will. Ironically something did happen during that century, and in England, that Keynes did not notice but somewhat favored the accumulation of capital in the hands of the entrepreneurial class: the expropriation of monasteries, carried out between 1534 and 1539 by Thomas Cromwell on behalf of Henry VIII— yes, he was into expropriating anything he could grab (Youings 1971;

Duffy 1992). But then, if Keynes had heard of it he would be ready to argue that the English Reformation was just a consequence of the Spanish bullion inflation.

Let us move on; even if the original accumulation did not come from the inflation of the sixteenth century, maybe it is true that it all started then and there. That is fine: forget the Hanseatic League, the Italian Comuni, the Netherlands, and all the rest; assume that capitalism started in England around 1580, as our Cambridge Don would like us to believe because it so pleases his ego. How did it continue? Compound interest, we are told: we, the civilized British people, stole the money from the Spaniards, invested it properly (mostly in colonial enterprises) and the power of compound interest did the rest. It is strange that the power of compound interest kicked in only in 1580— and indeed why would compound interest become effective and yield all this wealth if it were purely a matter of receiving interest from borrowers? Where does the REAL stuff come from? Adam Smith founded modern economics by exposing the fallacious mercantile idea that owning lots of gold and silver is a good thing for an economy. And English accumulation only begins with Drake's capture of a Spanish treasure in 1580! Can any human being suffer of monetary illusion more than this man did? No wonder he believed what he believed about the economic behavior of other humans, monetary illusion and all that: he was working through introspection. Keynes was guilty of the ultimate eurocentrism: he believed that our capital is what we invest abroad and its yield is what the "other guy" pays us. Our wealth is their poverty, our income is their loss. Fortunately three billion Chinese and Indians have learned otherwise, and so, whatever Keynes could have really meant, the virtuous cycle of physical production goes on.

Standing on the Shoulders of Giants

Standing on the shoulders of giants requires, sometimes, very good balancing skills. Keynes, we are told, was a giant of economics, so we have tried to stand on his large shoulders. We came up empty-handed, but we learned something about how not to theorize about human needs and their determinants.

That, possibly due to our "selfish genes," human desires are unlimited and that—despite the fact that it is always a limited set of "characteristics" we are seeking in goods and services—technological progress itself seems to offer an unbounded sequence of forms in which such characteristics can be satisfied, this we have also learned. How such desires evolve and how predictably we pursue them over time, we do not know. In fact we do not even know the extent to which the "animal impulses" inside ourselves determine our choices vis-à-vis the more rational, or calculating, pre-frontal cortex. We do not even reject the hypothesis that, maybe, our decision-making procedures are better modeled as a game between two of us, or two parts of our brains (Levine and Fudenberg 2006), as Keynes possibly meant to suggest with his metaphors of the brutish animal and the elevated spirit who can sing. We know we know little about this, but we do know this is something worth figuring out.

Bibliography

Boldrin, M., and D. K. Levine. 2002. Factor saving innovation. *Journal of Economic Theory* 105: 18–41.

Boldrin, M., and D. K. Levine. 2006. Quality ladders, competition and endogenous growth. Mimeo. Washington University in Saint Louis, October.

Cole, H., and L. Ohanian. 2002. The great U.K. depression: A puzzle and possible resolution. *Review of Economic Dynamics* 1: 19–44.

Crafts, N. 1999. Economic growth in the twentieth century. *Oxford Review of Economic Policy* 15: 18–34.

David, P. A., and G. Wright. 1999. Early twentieth century productivity growth dynamics: An inquiry into the economic history of "Our Ignorance." Mimeo. University of Oxford and Stanford University.

Diamond, J. 1997. *Guns, Germs and Steel: The Fates of Human Societies.* New York: Norton.

Duffy, E. 1992. *The Stripping of the Altars: Traditional Religion in England, 1400–1580.* New Haven: Yale University Press.

Fudenberg, D., and D. K. Levine. 2006. A dual self model of impulse control. *American Economic Review*, forthcoming.

Gali, J. 1999. Technology, employment, and the business cycle: Do technology shocks explain aggregate fluctuations? *American Economic Review* 89: 249–71.

Gordon, R. J. 2004. Two centuries of economic growth: Europe chasing the American frontier. Mimeo, Northwestern University.

Gordon, R. J. 2005. The 1920s and the 1990s in mutual reflection. Mimeo. Northwestern University.

Lane, F. C. 1963. The economic meaning of the invention of the compass. *American Historical Review* 68: 605–17.

McNeill, W. H. 1963. *The Rise of the West: A History of the Human Community.* Chicago: University of Chicago Press.

Mokyr, J. 1990. *The Lever of Riches: Technological Creativity and Economic Progress*. New York: Oxford University Press.

Rostovzev, M. 1926. *The Social and Economic History of the Roman Empire*. Oxford: Clarendon Press.

Solow, R. M. 1956. A contribution to the theory of economic growth. *Quarterly Journal of Economics* 70: 65–94.

Solow, R. M. 1957. Technical change and the aggregate production function. *Review of Economics and Statistics* 39: 312–20.

Trevor, W. I. 2000. *A History of Invention from Stone Axes to Silicon Chips*. New York: Facts on File.

Youings, J. 1971. *The Dissolution of the Monasteries*. London: Allen and Unwin.

13

Why Keynes Underestimated Consumption and Overestimated Leisure for the Long Run

Gary S. Becker and Luis Rayo

Keynes's short article, published in 1930, gives a remarkably optimistic, and in many ways prescient, assessment of the long-term economic future of the Western world, even while Britain and many other nations were immersed in a major depression. Keynes argues that the depression would be temporary, and that eventually growth would resume at the pace Britain and other nations in the economically advanced world had experienced since the early nineteenth century. That was a brave and in large measure accurate forecast of future growth over the long term. Actual British and American incomes have already grown some four- to fivefold since 1930 compared to Keynes's forecast of four- to eightfold increase by 2030. This is an excellent match, especially given the state of the economy in 1930.

We are impressed by the many insights crammed into this very short essay: the economic stagnation of the world until a couple of hundred years ago, the remarkable effects of compound interest on potential improvements in income, the importance of harnessing science to economic life to produce technological progress, the elimination of the need in the rich countries to toil hard just to acquire basic necessities, and still others. Yet Keynes went wrong in believing that the "economic" problem would disappear by 2030 if economic growth continues at the pace of the hundred years prior to his article. This outstanding economist was also mistaken in his expectations about the consequences of long-term growth for consumption and hours worked.

We highlight several problems in Keynes's discussion. These are principally his neglect of the positive implications for hours worked of the substitution effect induced by higher earnings, the difference between working habits of rich English gentlemen of his time and that of Americans and many other rich individuals working in different countries, the nature of the utility function that would be motivating most consumer behavior, his ignoring the possibility of future inventions of revolutionary goods and services in great demand by consumers, the nontrivial economic challenges involved in the allocation of time, including leisure time, and the economic advance of the vast majority of the world's population who then lived in mainly very poor countries. We discuss these issues partly in light of developments in economic analysis since Keynes wrote his essay almost eighty years ago.

Keynes assumed that higher incomes would lead to increased demand for leisure through what is now called the "income" effect. But in the same year as Keynes published this article, Lionel Robbins published a classic article showing that higher hourly earnings have conflicting effects on hours worked (Robbins 1930). The substitution effect leads to more work, whereas the income effect considered by Keynes reduces work. The net effect on hours worked depends on the utility function—for example, with a Cobb-Douglas function, hours worked are unaffected by permanent changes in wage rates. The empirical evidence also indicates that Cobb-Douglas is not a bad first approximation, at least after 1960, since average hours worked per adult between ages 18 and 65 have not declined much in response to the large increases in hourly earnings.

Keynes was misled in his predictions concerning the effect of higher income on hours worked by the behavior of gentlemen in Britain—who Keynes believed provided a window onto future behavior as everyone's income rose. Their behavior gave a distorted picture of what to expect because these gentlemen had sizable wealth in the form of physical and financial assets, but not high human capital or earnings. So economic theory would predict that these gentlemen would take more leisure than would equally wealthy persons in the future who in fact would be holding the vast majority of their wealth in human capital, rather than land and other assets. English gentlemen indeed had mainly just an income effect, while those who would have to work for their high incomes would also have powerful substitution effects.

This difference is illustrated by the working habits of wealthy individuals in the various Gulf States, who typically get the vast majority of their income from oil revenues. It is said that in many of these countries, such as the Emirates, Qatar, or Kuwait, the typical working day for natives—as opposed to the imported laborers who do not share in oil revenues—is about three to four hours a day. This is actually very close to Keynes's estimate of how many hours would be worked in advanced countries after another century of economic growth.

Modern research also indicates that utility of most individuals generally depends not on the absolute level of their consumption but rather on how large their consumption is relative to their past consumption, and relative also to the consumption of peers and other reference groups (a point only partially recognized by Keynes, as discussed below). To the extent that utility depends on reference points that ratchet up as income increases, individuals will always be striving for greater utility by trying to do better than they did in the past, and also by trying to keep up with their peers. This means that even a large growth in income does not automatically lead to satiation of consumption: as individuals strive to do better, they partly but never fully succeed since their reference points continue to rise along with their earning power.

Rayo and Becker (2007a, b) argue that humans evolved biologically so that they have reference points that adjust upward as their circumstances improve. In particular, their analysis implies that habits and peer influences would be major determinants of utility. They also show that this evolutionary model of utility is consistent with modern brain research. For example, analogous to utility, the human eye is specifically designed to measure light in relative, not absolute, terms (Kandel et al. 2000).

Interestingly Keynes also recognized the evolutionary origin of our drive to succeed: "we have been expressly evolved by nature—with all our impulses and deepest instincts—for the purpose of solving the economic problem." In addition he clearly recognized that human beings have needs that are "relative" in the sense that "we feel them only if their satisfaction lifts us above, makes us feel superior to, our fellows." And these needs, by definition, are insatiable: "for the higher the general level, the higher still are they." If Keynes had only placed more weight on our relative needs—and the fact that human nature is not easily changed—his predictions would have been radically different.

Central to Keynes's argument was his trust that at least our "absolute" needs, which we feel "whatever the situation of our fellow human beings may be," would eventually be satisfied. But he was also mistaken in this respect. Independently of peer influences, most types of material consumption are strongly habit-forming. After an initial period of excitement, the average consumer grows accustomed to what he has purchased, and perhaps driven by "natural purpose," he rapidly aspires to own the next product in line. Given these habits, even what Keynes called "absolute" needs may in fact be relative in nature—and therefore insatiable.

In addition Keynes paid essentially no attention to the likely development of revolutionary goods that would be greatly desired. This omission is especially surprising in light of Keynes's keen insights into the importance of technological progress in generating income growth. The three decades prior to his article saw the development of many goods that revolutionized living in the twentieth century: the invention of the light bulb, the electric motor, automobiles, airplanes, radio, and movies. Shortly after his article, came small washing machines, dryers, dishwashers, vacuum cleaners, television, and motorboats. Later came computers, videos, digital cameras, and cell phones, among many other consumer goods. The process of developing new goods that generate great demand continues unabated into the twenty-first century, and there is no obvious reason why this process should end. For example, if nothing else, it seems safe to expect that demand for medical advances and medical treatment will increase with no limit as income and technological developments continue to expand. After all, the desire for a longer, healthier life, is one that faces no bounds.

This discussion reveals a major blind spot in Keynes's approach to life. He correctly emphasized the future importance of technological advances that would raise the productivity of labor and capital, but he essentially ignored the potential creation of consumer goods that would continue to motivate individuals to have enough earnings to afford them.

Since Keynes believed that the "economic" problem would eventually largely disappear, and men and women would hardly have to work for a living, he concluded that we economists would become much less important. Of course, essentially the opposite has happened. For instance, no political candidate of any significance can now be without his or her coterie of economic advisors, and economists' opinions are constantly sought by the news media. Keynes went wrong partly because economists have greatly broadened their analysis beyond the material aspects of life to include subjects like happiness, altruism, social interactions, marriage and divorce, and others dealing with more nonmaterial aspects of life.

These developments indicate that Keynes defined "economics" much too narrowly. About the same time Keynes wrote this essay, Lionel Robbins also published his important 1932 book *An Essay on the Nature and Significance of Economic Science*, which took a far broader approach to "economics." Robbins's definition of the economic problem is the analysis of, and prescriptions for, the allocation of scarce means to competing ends. This definition includes the allocation of time outside of work, as well as between work and leisure. So even if Keynes had been right, and hours worked declined to a low level as income grew, a nontrivial economic problem would remain of how to allocate much larger levels of leisure time to various competing and time-absorbing activities. Keynes largely ignored the fact that time is the fundamental resource, and that time allocation requires serious economic analysis. Perhaps this omission simply reflects that he was not shy about prescribing what he considered to be the best way to use our leisure time. Apparently he considered that to be mainly a matter of valued and cultivated tastes that were outside the scope of economics.

Finally, Keynes showed little interest in this essay in the fact that, in 1930, about 90 percent of the world's population lived far below the standard of living in England, America, and a few other progressive countries. Indeed the standard of living in countries of Asia, Africa, Latin America, and elsewhere, was close to the low subsistence level that Keynes recognized was the lot of mankind until a couple of hundred years prior to his article. Thus, even if the economic problem, as Keynes defined it, disappeared in the few countries he was considering, economics would continue to be enormously important in analyzing the developing world.

Even though we have emphasized several blind spots in Keynes's article, we have done this with the benefit of hindsight—and the benefit of modern economic tools that were not available in Keynes's time. Few economists have been as productive as Keynes, and much progress in economic thought has been stimulated by the work of this innovative thinker.

Bibliography

Kandel, E. R., J. H. Schwartz, and T. M. Jessell. 2000. *Principles of Neural Science*. New York: McGraw-Hill.

Rayo, L., and G. S. Becker. 2007a. Evolutionary efficiency and happiness. *Journal of Political Economy* 115(2): 302–37.

Rayo, L., and G. S. Becker. 2007b. Habits, peers, and happiness: An evolutionary perspective. *American Economic Review, Papers and Proceedings* 97(2): 487–91.

Robbins, L. 1930. On the elasticity of demand for income in terms of effort. *Economica* 29: 123–29.

Robbins, L. 1932. *An Essay on the Nature and Significance of Economic Science.* New York: Macmillan.

14

What Is Wrong in Keynes's Prophecy? How the End of Economics Turned into the Rise of the Economics of Social Responsibility

Leonardo Becchetti

Predicting what humankind is going to be in the future is a fascinating but daunting task. Despite our theoretical and empirical progress in economics and in social sciences, we are able today, at best, of "doing good history" by interpreting and describing rigorously (with the help of statistics and econometrics) what has happened in the recent past. Whereas, as it is well known, our capacity to predict the near future is akin to that of car driver who decides what direction to take by looking out the rear window. This is all the more so for Keynes as the tools of social scientists in Keynes's age were much less sophisticated than today.

When there are no univocal coordinates for our prediction and vision of the future, the latter risk to become what we would like to see. It is therefore inevitable that when we dare to extend our scrutiny ahead in the future as far as the age of our grandchildren, we inevitably mix our inference with prejudices, ideals, and values. We suspect this has happened also for Keynes.

In evaluating Keynes's vision today, we must acknowledge some great intuitions (the growing and persistent role of technological progress in the future and the defeat of the Malthusian gloom prophecies, together with the reopening of the debate on the goal of human life and socioeconomic action due to the growing perceived importance of immaterial needs) together with less successful ones (the prediction of the progressive reduction of hours worked and of the end of economics—intended as the end or the much reduced relevance of economic problems).

In my comments to Keynes's short essay I will also highlight what are the missing elements that generated the wrong predictions and, inevitably, play the same game Keynes did by extending my look into the future. To resume in a few words my point, Keynes's immediate translation of higher aggregate affluence into social prosperity falls into the typical shortcut of assuming the existence of a benevolent planner doing that job. What is actually happening today is that the traditional system of check and balances, which was typically performing the task of reconciling economic development with social justice in the past, is in a state of crisis. The development and evolution of the new system of checks and balances will tell us whether we will be able to fulfill Keynes's prophecy about the end of economic problems.

The Successful Intuition: Enduring Technological Progress

We must acknowledge the great intuition of Keynes, who was able to extend his look beyond the Great Depression era in which he was living, and to identify it only as a temporary slowdown of a long-run trend of growth of per capita GDP, ensured by the sustained and persistent pace of technical progress.

From its "time-constrained" point of view, Keynes could not see the information and communications technological revolution looming at the horizon, but even without seeing it, his confidence in the relentless march of technical progress leads him to predict that the wave of innovations would proceed (despite the Great Depression) and ensure increasing welfare to humankind. As is well known, we witness today an incredible acceleration of this process determined by the wave of innovations in the electronic and telecommunication industry known as information and communication technology (or ICT). This stream of technological advancements has dramatically reduced the cost and increased the speed at which everything "weightless" (e.g., voice, images, data, and music) may be transferred across distant places in the world. To make an astounding example, as is well known, in 1979 it took us almost 7 hours and 800 dollars to fly from Rome to New York. The situation is almost the same today (with some bounces back since the Concord is not flying anymore…). If time and cost of transport of what has a weight had followed the trend of what is weightless, we should be able to fly to New York today in less than a second by paying less than a penny! Despite this enlarged gap in innovation in the two areas, the technical progress in the speed of microprocessors and competition in the computer industry has rapidly spread ICT as a multipurpose innovation capable of dramatically improving productivity in all fields of industry and human life.

Such a revolution, and the sustained pace of technical progress before it, produced the miracle of an increase in population in less than a century never witnessed in the past (from 1.5 billion to more than 6 billion). Even though we still have around 1 billion people below the absolute poverty line (without tackling the issue of the complexity of the calculation of such a threshold), the last decades were able to ensure decent life to around 4.5 billion neonates. Yet distributional bottlenecks do not allow us to extend prosperity to all human beings, as would be possible given the economic value created at the aggregate and the global level.

The Wrong Intuition: The Reduction of Worked Hours and the Anthropological Fallacy

The question then is what went wrong with some of Keynes's intuitions. The most unfortunate is that technical progress would have led to an almost jobless age in which the dramatic increase in productivity would allow humankind to produce what is needed in much fewer worked hours, thereby dedicating much more time to leisure. To be more precise in addressing this issue, we need to decide whether this prediction is substantially incorrect or, alternatively, is correct in the long run, and it is just a question of time before we see happening what Keynes had envisaged.

My strong belief is that this specific prediction of Keynes is driven by a crucial "anthropological fallacy." Keynes's vision of labor is too much influenced by the Marxist concept of alienation and framed in the specific perspective of economic textbook "manual workers." To broaden this perspective consider that the main difference between the Marxist conception and that of the Christian Social Doctrine is that, for the former, work is only alienation whereas for the second, it has two dimensions. The first (objective) dimension is still alienating and painful but has a sense on its own, given that man realizes himself also by carrying such a burden. The second (subjective) dimension is creative and emphasizes that, through his job, man continues and perfects God's work of creation.

By keeping in mind these two perspectives, if we look at most formalizations or theoretical thinking in labor economics, and at those prevailing in Keynes's age, they are quite close to the Marxian perspective. The individual chooses the optimal allocation of his hours between work and leisure. Work does not produce any enjoyment and, in standard formalizations, is accompanied by an immaterial cost represented by the disutility of effort. Such disutility, or lack of utility, is compensated by a monetary reward (the wage), which is used to enjoy consumption goods in the leisure time. It is therefore clear that if we stick to this vision, which we must understand as greatly influenced by the prevalence of alienating tasks in Keynes's time, we are likely to expect that the "alienated" *homo oeconomicus* should try to exploit increased productivity and hourly wages to reduce worked hours, or in other terms, that income effects should dominate substitution effects.

The anthropological fallacy by which Keynes is affected is that of considering only the alienating component of human work without considering its positive side, consisting in the realization of the human creative dimension and, even, in the deep value and motivation of his physical sacrifice. In simpler words, if Keynes were to have been a psychologist working today on the mental depression of many white-collar workers soon after their retirement, he would have had a clearer vision of this missed positive dimension of human work.

But Keynes was wrong not just because we cannot merely live off leisure and instead find pleasure in our jobs (at least in those professions that are less alienating and more gratifying) but also because we need to work even after great technical revolutions are ensuring us a growing amount of goods and services. We need to work because the pace of technological progress needs to be sustained by our creativity but also because we need professionals to organize the fruition of our leisure (i.e., leisure and entertainment is an industry in itself creating many jobs). If we slightly correct Keynes's prediction from that on overall worked hours to that of hours worked in the production of material goods, we come to be almost correct. Just consider how, today, the share of manufacturing on GDP is around 20 percent or lower (it was much higher in Keynes's time), whereas the share of services to the industrial sector or of the leisure industry is progressively increasing.

The great miracle that even Keynes's optimism could not envisage is the transformation of jobs and of value-creating activities in our economies, with the progressive reduction of alienating works in the production of physical goods, and the parallel expansion of production of "ecologically lighter" nonrival goods or services in the fields of art, leisure, and entertainment. This transformation will make it easier in the future to maintain significant growth rates, while framing them in an ecologically and socially sustainable perspective (given the more parsimonious use of environmental resources) and reducing the share of alienating tasks, thereby increasing the enjoyment associated with human enterprise.

If we just reflect on some of the "productive activities" that are dominant today, we can really see how much this change has happened. In the past people had to perform hard work and talked about sports or futile issues in their free time. Nowadays barroom discussions have turned to professional activity, tunnelled into successful TV programs and drawing millions of people to them. In parallel, we have the industries of gossip, of holiday village entertainment, and so on. I am, of course, aware that at the moment the North–South division of labor is not equally allocating the benefits of this transformation, but I am confident that, as far as the process of conditional convergence proceeds, also this imbalance will be progressively reduced.

A fallacy in the anthropological vision of human work and the incapacity of understanding the evolution of jobs and value-creating activities are at the root of Keynes's misleading notion about the future of worked hours.

Absolutely Satiable and Relatively Insatiable Wants: From Growth to "Economically Sustainable Happiness"

Part of Keynes's analysis revolves around the evolution of human needs in this process of increasing prosperity. The point of Keynes is that absolute needs will be satisfied by economic growth and technological progress while it will be impossible to do the same for relative ones. In another crucial passage Keynes argues that the economic problem (related to the satisfaction of absolute needs) will be solved. If this is going to occur, the cultural background developed to stimulate creation of economic value will not be necessary anymore, and the main problem will be a different one, namely adaptation to the new scenario and capacity to enjoy immaterial and spiritual goods.

Again, in this framework we find more successful and less successful intuitions. Among the former, we find the distinction between absolute and relative needs, where relative ones are those more complex to satisfy. A second brilliant point is the identification of a cultural dimension, superstructural in the Marxian sense, that produces those values that are instrumental and functional to support economic progress of humankind at a given stage of its evolution. If we think of the importance of duty and sacrifice in the culture of just some decades ago, and how these values have partially disappeared in our times, we understand that this intuition is profound. Keynes develops it by making reference to a cultural value that is functional to the goal of sustaining workers' productivity, the value of money accumulation considered as an end in itself and not as a mean to pursue immaterial and superior goals. In this sense Keynes's argument is close to the Smithian "deception" argument where philosophers know that productive activity is not the ultimate driver of human happiness, but they consciously deceive the masses because the materialist ranking of values is necessary to stimulate the creation of material goods that are necessary for the well-being of higher classes (Smith 1759).

In this perspective, I believe that the era of deceit is going to end because we are at the eve of a great change that is also reflecting on the way economics is going to be conceived in the near future. The evolution of aspirations in people that are always more free from needs (at least in some parts of the world) will probably bring in a modification in the conception of the *homo oeconomicus* and of our objective function. Such modification is needed if economists aim to give successful advice to politicians. The pursuit of purely economic goals (GDP growth), which may eventually trade off immaterial goods such as quality of human relationships, may generate, in this modified framework, the paradoxical effect of a drop in political consensus with richer but less happy electors that are going to punish and not to praise their governments in charge. Politicians who depend on it will be the first to require this change of perspective from economists. The new economics of happiness is born for this purpose and is attracting ever more and more research (Alesina et al. 2001; Bruni et al. 2004; Clark 1994; Frey et al. 2000; Layard 2005).

What made possible this renaissance of happiness studies is the novelty of the collection of ample and detailed empirical information on self-declared happiness at the individual level for most of the world countries. We tend to use this empirical evidence to test hypotheses stemming from theoretical model derivations, but we should also use it to test whether crucial assumptions, on which our models rely, are sound. The available evidence on self-declared happiness gives us the unique opportunity of verifying whether the way we build our utility function is correct. Results, available for different countries and different sample periods, clearly show that the assumption of self-interested individuals maximizing the level of their consumption is clearly untenable.

We imagine ourselves as "rational fools," but hopefully, we do not succeed in transforming ourselves as such. Empirical evidence on happiness and empirical "anomalies" that reject the *homo oeconomicus* restrictive assumptions seem to confirm Sen's (1977) famous critique arguing that, together with self-interest, we have the two fundamental dimensions of sympathy and commitment, both having strong influence on our behavior. This helps us understand why empirical studies on happiness show that immaterial values, such as the time spent enjoying relationships, religious practice, education, and health are so important for people in any part of the world.

It is also worth trying to frame the role of money in a different perspective, as a means and not as an end in itself, as Keynes correctly argued. Happiness studies are almost univocal in telling us that even though we must not neglect the fact that personal and domestic affluence may be crucial to achieve superior goods, such as quality of education and health, we must equally be aware that happiness is not at all monotonically increasing in personal income. The relationship between the two variables is much more complex and depends on relative affluence with respect to the reference group (the sociological dimension) and from the complex dynamics of achievements and aspirations (the psychological dimension), where the latter become inevitably higher every time a new peak has been climbed. Furthermore some of the most recent studies disclose a potential negative indirect effect of income on happiness, the so-called Baumol disease of relational goods (Becchetti-Santoro 2006). The problem is that as we become more productive, the opportunity cost of leisure becomes higher. Unfortunately, the "productivity" of human relationships does not grow at all, or does not grow apace with productivity in manufacturing (we must dedicate the same amount of hours as ever to develop a friendship or to raise children if we believe that cell-phone conversations cannot replace other kinds of human contacts...). Hence we require time to develop friendships or to invest in different types of relational goods (family ties, development of clubs or association, organization of a football match among friends, etc.). Unfortunately, relational goods are "local public goods" that require the joint investment of individuals who are both producers and consumers of these goods at the same time (family or club members). Hence, as productivity grows, the risk of coordination failure grows because individuals with stronger preferences for relational goods may end up being less happy if their peers, who should co-produce and co-consume the relational goods, do not share the same preferences. Far from what was predicted by Keynes, what we are facing today as a consequence of the increasing productivity is not the reduction of worked hours but a deterioration of the quality of relational goods.

Empirical evidence on this point is significant. The effect of the time spent in relationships with friends, family members, members of different types of association, is a robust and positive determinant of individual happiness (Becchetti, Londono Bedoya, and Trovato 2006). In turn a negative relationship exists, at individual and country levels, between income and enjoyment of relational goods.

This evidence confirms and provides new insights for a well-known saying: Individuals in our societies are rich in money and poor in time, while those in less affluent societies are poor in money but richer in time.

To sum up, we may refine Keynes's intuition here by arguing that individuals tend to be always more and more aware of the importance of immaterial goods as their income grows and as they realize that the relationship between the latter and their happiness is definitely not ever increasing. They start demanding more immaterial goods, and "enlightened" politicians understand that *homo oeconomicus* based recipes are not enough to make them win the next elections.

With Work Still Necessary and Distributional Conflicts Not Yet Solved, How Do We Square the Circle?

A main limit of Keynes's arguments is the idea that the unstopping pace of technological advancement would automatically solve the economic problem. Actually he admits that to fulfill this dream, some side conditions need to be met, such as "power to control population, determination to avoid wars and civil dissensions, willingness to entrust to science . . . ." In this list two issues are missing: environmental sustainability and the idea that distributional problems arise as productivity grows and remains concentrated in a few hands.

Beyond Keynes's cursory reference to "avoid civil dissension" (or social conflict) there are the crucial questions of environmental and social sustainability of economic development in globally integrated markets. The problem that economists need to address is not just the aggregate amount of production generated in a given unit of time but also the negative externalities and distributional conflicts that this level of production may generate. The ICT revolution and economic global integration have actually increased interdependences among once distant regions and have made more urgent the problem of market failures (insufficient production of public goods, negative environmental externalities, inequality in starting conditions, etc.). The simplistic approach of Keynes mirrors the heroic assumptions of those economic models in which representative individuals hide all distributional problems and perfectly informed benevolent planners successfully bridge the gap between individual and social optimum bypassing conflicts of interest and informational asymmetries.

What is happening in reality is that global market integration has weakened the old system of checks and balances that was based on the interaction among three actors. According to the previous system, on the one side, corporations created economic value but also negative externalities, on the other side, powerful domestic institutions and trade unions acted to address and correct these imbalances. The old "three-pillar" system has fallen into pieces as corporations have started moving into a globalized scenario in which domestic institutions and trade unions have much less bargaining power (due to government fiscal competition and competition of labor costs generated by the option of delocalization). A new system of global checks and balances has actually raised "civil dissension" (to use Keynes's words), even within a framework of rising global prosperity. In this new framework the economic system has been able to produce endogenous temporary defenses with the rise of a new important actor: the civil society. In this vacuum of global rules and institutions, a minority of concerned individuals started to vote with their portfolios, using consumption and savings to promote those corporations that were more innovative in terms of socially responsible action. The old three-pillar system has therefore been replaced by a new one in which the weakness of domestic trade unions has been compensated by the vicarious action of concerned consumers and investors.

The rise of the phenomenon of corporate social responsibility is just the result of this bottom-up pressure. In the last decade social pressure assisted the significant growth of so-called socially responsible investments in terms of the volumes brokered by financial intermediaries. According to the 2003 Report on Socially Responsible Investing Trends in the United States (downloadable at *http://www.socialinvest.org/ resources/research/*) the stock of ethically managed mutual fund assets reached $2.16 trillion in the same year if one includes all US private and institutional ethically screened portfolios. Based on these figures, one out of nine dollars under professional management in the United States was invested in socially responsible portfolios. On the consumption side, the 2003 Corporate Social Responsibility Monitor (downloadable at *http://www.bsdglobal.com/issues/sr.asp*) finds that the proportion of consumers looking at social responsibility in their choices jumped from 36 percent in 1999 to 62 percent in 2001 in Europe. Research undertaken in February 2004 by the German market research company TNS Emnid on a representative sample of the population finds that 2.9 percent of those interviewed buy fair trade products regularly (Becchetti Rosati 2007), 19 percent rarely, and 6 percent almost never. Of the respondents 35 percent said they support the idea but do not buy these products (*www.fairtrade.net/sites/aboutflo/aboutflo*). In a parallel UK survey, Bird and Hughes (1997) classify consumers as ethical (24 percent), semi-ethical (57 percent), and self-interested (19 percent). Of the surveyed consumers 18 percent declared to be willing to pay a premium for socially responsible products. In the light of these important changes, it should not come as a surprise that for the 2005 KPMG report, 52 percent of the top 100 corporations in the 16 more industrialized countries published a corporate social responsibility (CSR) report.

The stimulus for corporations to adopt a more socially responsible stance does not come only from the bottom-up action of socially responsible consumers and investors. Costs of paying greater attention to the interests of workers, subcontractors, local communities, or future generations when choosing CSR may be compensated by at least three potential benefits, beyond that of the support of concerned individuals: (1) the minimization of conflicts with stakeholders (Freeman 1984) and therefore of costs of litigation and legal actions, (2) the opportunity of signaling product quality in a framework of asymmetric information between sellers and buyers, above all in those sectors (e.g., the food industry or the banking system) where the consequences of purchasing "lemons" may be more serious for consumers, and (3) the positive effect of CSR on workers motivation and therefore on their productivity. The last point is quite promising and deserves to be investigated in more detail in the future. To shed light on this point, just consider how the most recent surveys in labor economics and personnel management (Baker, Jensen, and Murphy 1998; Baker, Gibbons, and Murphy 2002) emphasize how, in the move from the Taylorist to the modern and more creative way of production, intrinsic motivations are always more crucial in triggering the extra creativity of workers, which may generate product and process innovation and new varieties of goods.

The emerging economics of social responsibility tells us a few important things. First, the centrality of consumption suggests us that the Marxian idea of an external social conflict (between capitalists and workers) is transformed into a new "internal" conflict between our working and consuming selves. This is because corporations depend on consumer choices, and in many cases, below a certain threshold of price there is a welfare improvement of our second dimension (that of consumers) at the cost of a humiliation of the first dimension (that of workers). Second, the market for socially responsible products suggests that not all individuals consume (invest) on the basis of the lowest price (or of the highest risk-adjusted return), documenting that self-interest cannot explain all economic behavior. Third, the dichotomy between the moment of creation of economic value (which generates negative externalities and distributional conflicts) and that of redistribution (which corrects them) may be avoided in principle if, under the principles of CSR, economic value is created in a more socially and environmentally responsible way. Fourth, a new type of economic agent, the market social enterprise, is born. The market social enterprise is a step beyond the dichotomous alternative between corporations, which create economic value and maximize shareholders wealth, on the one side, and those not-for-profit organizations that fulfill social goals but do not create economic value. Market social enterprises (fair trade producers, microfinance institutions, etc.) but also traditional corporations moving from the goal of maximizing shareholders wealth to that of satisfying the interests of a wider set of stakeholders (workers, local communities, component producers, etc.) fill an important gap in the economic system by creating both economic and social value, and by creating economic value in a more socially and environmentally responsible way, that internalizes their potential negative externalities.

Conclusions

Keynes's vision of the future for our grandchildren discloses great intuition but not without some fallacies. We are neither at the end of history, nor at the end of labor and economics. The astounding pace of technological progress creates new opportunities but also new challenges. Economic value creation per unit of time is continuing to rise, but this is not enough to solve our economic problems. What Keynes took for granted in his prophecy is that the system of checks and balances would have transformed the higher aggregate affluence into an acceptably equitable social outcome, necessary to avoid "civil dissension." What he did not foresee is that global market integration has significantly weakened that system of checks and balances, pushing the economic system to produce new endogenous defenses under the form of the new phenomenon of the economics of social responsibility.

If the toll of labor is not to be removed from our shoulders, the economics of social responsibility and the rise of market social enterprises—by pressing human entrepreneurship toward the higher goal of the pursuit of social inclusion and less toward material goods—may reconcile the need to solve social and environmental imbalances and the dream of making our productive effort less humiliating and more rewarding.

Bibliography

Alesina, A., R. Di Tella, and R. MacCulloch. 2001. Inequality and happiness: Are Europeans and Americans different? NBER working paper 8198. Cambridge, MA.

Baker, G., R. Gibbons, and K. J. Murphy. 2002. Relational contracts and the theory of the firm. *Quarterly Journal of Economics* 117(1): 39–84.

Baker, G., M. C. Jensen, and K. J. Murphy. 1998. Compensation and incentives: Practive vs. theory. *Journal of Finance* 63(3): 593–616.

Becchetti, L., D. Londono Bedoya, and G. Trovato. 2006. Income, relational goods and happiness. CEIS working paper 227.

Becchetti, L., and M. Santoro. 2006. The wealth-unhappiness paradox: A relational goods/Baumol disease explanation. In L. Bruni and L. La Porta, eds., *Handbook of Happiness in Economics*, London: Elgar.

Becchetti, L., and F. Rosati. 2007. Globalization and the death of distance in social preferences and inequity aversion: Empirical evidence from a pilot study on fair trade consumers. *World Economy* 30(5): 807–30.

Bird, K., and D. Hughes. 1997. Ethical consumerism: The case of "fairly-traded" coffee. *Business Ethics: A European Review* 6(3): 159–67.

Bruni, L., and P. L. Porta. 2004. *Felicità ed Economia*. Milano: Guerini associati.

Clark, A. E., and A. J. Oswald. 1994. Unhappiness and unemployment. *Economic Journal, Royal Economic Society* 104(424): 648–59.

Corporate Social Responsibility Monitor. 2003. Available at ⟨http://www.bsdglobal .com/issues/sr.asp⟩.

Duesenberry, J. 1949. *Income, Saving and the Theory of Consumer Behaviour*. Cambridge: Harvard University Press.

Easterlin, R. A. 2001. Income and happiness: Towards a unified theory. *Economic Journal* 111: 465–84.

Fehr, E., and A. Falk. 2002. Psychological foundations of incentives. *European Economic Review* 46: 687–724.

Frank, R. H. 1997. The frame of reference as a public good. *Economic Journal* 107(445): 1832–47.

Freeman, R. E. 1984. *Strategic Management: A Stakeholder approach*. Boston: Pitman.

Frey, B. S., and A. Stutzer. 2000. Happiness, economy and institutions. *Economic Journal* 110: 918–38.

KPMG International Survey of Corporate Responsibility Reporting 2005. Available at ⟨www.kpmg.com/Rut2000_prod/Documents/9/Survey2005.pdf⟩.

Report on Socially Responsible Investing Trends in the United States. 2003. Available at ⟨http://www.socialinvest.org/resources/research⟩.

Sen, A. 1977. Rational fools: A critique of the behavioral foundations of economic theory. *Philosophy and Public Affairs* 6(4): 317–44.

Smith, A. [1759] 1984. *The Theory of Moral Sentiments*. London, pp. 182–85.

15

Really Thinking Long Run: Keynes's Other Masterpiece

William J. Baumol

Economic analysis offers us weapons like the Ricardian growth model that are designed to help us think about the very long run—about the wonders that history has achieved and what it promises for the future. But few of us take the bait. Economists are all too prone to provide forecasts for the next few months, or even a year or two ahead. Economists' record at this is not quite brilliant, so it should come as no surprise that, seventy-five years after John Maynard Keynes undertook to look a century ahead, it is clear that much of what he foretold then will not come to pass. But, as I will argue here, his misjudgments are as illuminating as his valid observations.

I am in no position to complain about erroneous predictions. On the many occasions when I have been asked for an economic forecast, my response has been that my only prediction about the future is that it will surprise me.[1] But in the essay under discussion, Keynes's observations about the distant past are so remarkable—and the poor predictions that emerged from his clouded telescope so illuminating—that we must forgive him his many sins, not only for his outright errors but even his then-fashionable anti-Semitism. Accordingly, in this chapter I will undertake to praise Caesar, not to bury him (or rather, his predictions). That is, I will not seek to point out the source of Keynes's errors nor to offer a forecast of my own—one that, I would dare to suggest there is reason to believe, will fare better than his. After all, who can lay plausible claims to qualification as a seer or can even claim to have undisputable explanations of the past? Is there, even today, a unique and certain account of any past economic phenomenon such as one of the depressions of the nineteenth century?

Keynes on the Distant Past: Prehistoric Breakthrough Invention

Let me begin with the past—with two of Keynes's observations that must lead us to reevaluate standard conclusions that are usually taken to be nearly self-evident and largely beyond dispute. I will decide that the standard conclusions remain valid, but that they must be regarded with a soupçon of modesty, that is, with a bit less unalloyed confidence.

The first of these matters is the uniqueness of the achievements of "the" industrial revolution and its sequel, as well as our intuitive grasp of the magnitude of those achievements. The second relates to possible explanations of the ensuing growth in per capita wealth accumulation. With good reason, we think of the innovative accomplishments of the past two centuries as something unparalleled in human history. When before has humanity been able to travel so fast or so far, to hear the voices and see the faces of its ancestors, or to communicate instantly with someone at the opposite end of the world? When before has real per capita GDP nearly octupled in one century? All this is often said, but is extremely difficult to digest and comprehend (a topic to which I will return presently). Yet the point I want to make here is that Keynes already provides a major insight in his caveat on this conclusion:

The absence of important technical inventions between the prehistoric age and comparatively modern times is truly remarkable. Almost everything which really matters and which the world possessed at the commencement of the modern age was already known to man at the dawn of history. Language, fire, the same domestic animals which we have to-day, wheat, barley, the vine and the olive, the plough, the wheel, the oar, the sail, leather, linen and cloth, bricks and pots, gold and silver, copper, tin, and lead—and iron was added to the list before 1000 B.C.—banking, statecraft, mathematics, astronomy, and religion. There is no record of when we first possessed these things.

At some epoch before the dawn of history—perhaps even in one of the comfortable intervals before the last ice age—there must have been an era of progress and invention comparable to that in which we live to-day.

This passage certainly is effective in suggesting the need for a sense of proportion in our thinking. We and our immediate ancestors did not inaugurate the accumulation of breakthrough inventions. Arguably, many of those that Keynes lists—as contributions that apparently appeared out of nowhere—can be taken to dwarf virtually any of those of the past two centuries. But there is something to be said on the other side. That prehistoric period since humankind, fully evolved, had first made its appearance, up until the first recording of historic events and characters, spans more than 100,000 years. The inventions and discoveries on Keynes's list add up to some 20 items. Assuming that these were meant merely to be suggestive, and that a defensible list with 100 such entries can be put together, means that in the period at issue, on average, one breakthrough appeared every thousand years. That is hardly what we would take to be an outpouring of inventive contributions. Of course, we may yet be surprised—archeologists constantly encounter surprises in this arena, as in others, finding complex Greek toothed gears and Chinese instruments of mass production, but neither of these examples is prehistoric. A Stone Age era of invention at anything like the nineteenth century pace is hardly very plausible.

Keynes on Post-Renaissance Accumulation

With good reason, we credit the bulk of the achievement since the Industrial Revolution—in terms of growing incomes and accumulating wealth—to rising productivity, primarily taken to be attributable to the inventors, the scientists, the entrepreneurs, and perhaps the educators of the modern era. But Keynes offers another startling observation, which does not negate this conclusion but should surely give us pause. It is an evaluation of the conceivable size of the portion of post-Renaissance economic growth that could have been achieved by mere accumulation.

... the power of compound interest over two hundred years is such as to stagger the imagination.

Let me give an illustration of this a sum which I have worked out. The value of Great Britain's foreign investments to-day is estimated at about £4,000 million. This yields us an income at the rate of about $6\frac{1}{2}$ per cent. Half of this we bring home and enjoy; the other half, namely, $3\frac{1}{4}$ per cent, we leave to accumulate abroad at compound interest. Something of this sort has now been going on for about 250 years.

For I trace the beginnings of British foreign investment to the treasure which Drake stole from Spain in 1580. In that year he returned to England bringing with him the prodigious spoils of the *Golden Hind*. Queen Elizabeth was a considerable shareholder in the syndicate which had financed the expedition. Out of her share she paid off the whole of England's foreign debt, balanced her Budget, and found herself with about £40,000 in hand.... Now it happens that £40,000 accumulating at 3 percent compound interest approximately corresponds to the actual volume of England's foreign investments at various dates, and would actually amount today to the total of £4,000 million which I have already quoted as being what our foreign investments now are. Thus, every £1 which Drake brought home in 1580 has now become £100,000. Such is the power of compound interest.

None of this means that mere accumulation achieved all or even most of the growth miracle of the past few centuries. It seems quite clear instead that invention merits the primary place as the fundamental source of the growth accomplishment. I interpret Keynes at this point merely to be drawing attention to the enormous power of accumulation and compounding. We all recognize this mechanism but tend not to grasp the incredible magnitude of its force. Keynes's argument can be extended. According to Angus Maddison's (2003) rather conservative estimate, during the twentieth century, British real per capita GDP rose by a multiple of approximately 4.5 (that of the United States rose nearly sevenfold). We may note that the British figure is right in the range in Keynes's forecast. In the same period British total real GDP rose by a multiple of 6.5.

But if the initial (1900) figures had risen at the rate cited by Keynes— 3.25 percent per annum, over the century, with compounding—they would have increased about 25 times! Of course, this does not make irrelevant the contributions from the inputs that are usually taken to underlay productivity growth. No nation does or can place its entire wealth in a bank account yielding a steady 3.25 percent, nor could any bank account have offered such a *real* rate of return without the growth of productivity contributed by the sweat of the brow and the exercise of the mind. Still it does suggest, as Keynes points out, that sheer investment has contributed more to the growth miracle than is currently credited to it. It implies that any recipe for really substantial growth should call for a significant saving rate, somehow elicited when no Keynesian recession is on the horizon, so that the saving will not impede growth rather than magnifying it as only accumulation may be able to do.

On Assessment of Incomprehensible Magnitudes: The Value of the Erroneous Forecasts

The most obvious observations on a first reading of Keynes's essay are the mistakes in what he presages:

Now for my conclusion, which you will find, I think, to become more and more startling to the imagination the longer you think about it.

I draw the conclusion that, assuming no important wars and no important increase in population, the *economic problem* may be solved, or be at least within sight of solution, within a hundred years. This means that the economic problem is not—if we look into the future—*the permanent problem of the human race.*

Why, you may ask, is this so startling? It is startling because—if, instead of looking into the future, we look into the past—we find that the economic problem, the struggle for subsistence, always has been hitherto the primary, most pressing problem of the human race—not only of the human race, but of the whole of the biological kingdom from the beginnings of life in its most primitive forms.

Keynes goes on to offer an evaluation of the prospect:

Will this be a benefit? . . . [F]or the first time since his creation man will be faced with his real, his permanent problem—how to use his freedom from pressing economic cares, how to occupy the leisure, which science and compound interest will have won for him, to live wisely and agreeably and well. . . .

Yet there is no country and no people, I think, who can look forward to the age of leisure and of abundance without a dread. For we have been trained too long to strive and not to enjoy. It is a fearful problem for the ordinary person, with no special talents, to occupy himself, especially if he no longer has roots in the soil or in custom or in the beloved conventions of a traditional society. . . .

For many ages to come the old Adam will be so strong in us that everybody will need to do some work if he is to be contented. We shall do more things for ourselves than is usual with the rich to-day, only too glad to have small duties and tasks and routines. But beyond this, we shall endeavour to spread the bread thin on the butter—to make what work there is still to be done to be as widely shared as possible. Three-hour shifts or a fifteen-hour week may put off the problem for a great while. For three hours a day is quite enough to satisfy the old Adam in most of us![2]

Three-hour workdays! Intolerable boredom! Total elimination of poverty throughout the world (surely the meaning of solution of the economic problem)! How different this is from the reality of the onset of the twenty-first century. How could Keynes have gone so wrong? Although that is not my point, as we will see, there are a number of explanations ready to hand. There have indeed been wars since 1930, wars whose destructiveness may well have exceeded anything experienced before the twentieth century. And there has been a flood of innovative products, television, computers, and many others that consumers found irresistible (at least after stimulation by abundant advertising), and found it necessary to work long enough to pay for them.

But even if these explanations are right and nearly adequate, does it imply that we are better equipped than Keynes to provide valid prognostications for the century that follows today? I very much doubt that, particularly given the prospect of global climate change and the growing availability of weapons of mass destruction at bargain prices.

The misjudgment of Keynes is helpful to us for an entirely different reason. Not because it teaches us to become better prophets. Patently it does not. Rather, what it helps us to do is to give ourselves and others the beginnings of a sense of the magnitude of what recent centuries have brought to the more fortunate nations and the more fortunate of their inhabitants. As reported above, in the United States, real per capita income has increased by a factor of nearly seven in the century that has recently concluded.

I maintain, particularly on the basis of recent experience, that this is a change so enormous that it is virtually impossible to comprehend. In numerous lectures on entrepreneurship and growth, I have tried repeatedly to give audiences a sense of the magnitude of this miracle. I have described indicators of the old ways of living: for example, that in most households in the nineteenth century ink was expected to freeze in the inkwells every winter, and that in much of continental Europe famine and widespread starvation were experienced about once a decade until at least the seventeenth century. I have emphasized that our forebears (perhaps with exceptions like Jules Verne and H. G. Wells) could not have imagined today's luxuries, which are now almost universally available. I have called attention to revolutionary inventions that could only have been explained as acts of magic to our ancestors (and perhaps even to ourselves). I have challenged my listeners to undertake the following thought experiment: Imagine that you have the income and wealth of an average American today and that suddenly six dollars out of every seven is removed from your wages, your bank account and every other money supply that is available to you. Can you envision what your life would then be like? The response has usually seemed to be somewhat uncomprehending acknowledgment. I have never felt that my effort had produced the desired insights. Indeed I must admit that despite my investment of substantial effort, I *myself* have never really succeeded in meeting that challenge of comprehension.

But now Keynes's failed foresight offers me a new way to go about the task. My approach had been to try to get the audiences to look backward, to envision what life was really like a century earlier. The natural reaction, surely, is that it could not really have been all that bad. After all, our ancestors did survive and did not feel themselves to be living in abject poverty. Indeed they were well enough to contribute to our own appearance. Now Keynes has offered me a new and promising approach to effective explanation: a forward-looking challenge, rather than a challenge to look backward. I can now ask the audience to suppose that real US income will once again increase sevenfold in the next century. Can you imagine what luxuries average-earning Americans will then have at their disposal? And perhaps I can then stimulate their thinking further by recalling Keynes's failure as a prophet. Surely that will help get my point across.[3]

Notes

1. I learned my lesson the hard way when I predicted in 1936 that Alfred Landon would win the American presidency against Franklin D. Roosevelt. The reader may recall that FDR's subsequent victory was one of the greatest landsides in US history. This experience led me to excessive caution. When, in our 1966 book on the economics of the performing arts, William Bowen and I laid out the cost disease theory and, on it, based projections that have proved qualitatively accurate for forty years, I was too cowardly to label our numbers as a forecast (see Baumol and Bowen 1966, especially pp. 405–407).

2. Or, as Henry Ford is reported to have put the matter, "The unhappiest man on earth, is the one who has nothing to do" (cited in Landes 2006, p. 132).

3. But this thought experiment will not work so easily if we take Keynes to have been right in his prognostication. For if humanity were to react to growing prosperity as he foresaw, the pace of output growth will be far less than it has been, and the benefits instead will consist predominantly of immeasurable psychic and aesthetic pleasures whose magnitude will be far less obvious and even far less definable than a continuing explosion of output and innovation.

Bibliography

Baumol, W. J., and W. G. Bowen. 1966. *Performing Arts: The Economic Dilemma.* New York: Twentieth Century Fund.

Keynes, J. M. 1930. *Economic Possibilities for our Grandchildren* (chapter 1, this volume).

Landes, D. S. 2006. *Dynasties.* New York: Viking.

Maddison, A. 2003. *The World Economy: Historical Statistics.* Paris: OECD.

Index